A Cook's Alphabet
of Quotations

A Cook's Alphabet
of Quotations

EDITED BY
MARIA POLUSHKIN ROBBINS

A DUTTON BOOK

DUTTON
Published by the Penguin Group
Penguin Books USA Inc., 375 Hudson Street,
New York, New York 10014, U.S.A.
Penguin Books Ltd, 27 Wrights Lane, London W8 5TZ, England
Penguin Books Australia Ltd, Ringwood, Victoria, Australia
Penguin Books Canada Ltd, 10 Alcorn Avenue,
Toronto, Ontario, Canada M4V 3B2
Penguin Books (N.Z.) Ltd, 182–190 Wairau Road, Auckland 10, New Zealand

Penguin Books Ltd, Registered Offices:
Harmondsworth, Middlesex, England

First published by Dutton, an imprint of New American Library,
a division of Penguin Books USA Inc.
Distributed in Canada by McClelland & Stewart Inc.

First Printing, October, 1991
10 9 8 7 6 5 4 3 2 1

 REGISTERED TRADEMARK—MARCA REGISTRADA

LIBRARY OF CONGRESS CATALOGING IN PUBLICATION DATA:

Polushkin, Maria.
    A cook's alphabet of quotations / Maria Polushkin Robbins.
        p.   cm.
    Includes index.
    ISBN 0-525-93359-X
    1. Quotations, English. 2. Food—Quotations, maxims, etc.
3. Food—Humor. 4. Cookery—Quotations, maxims, etc. I. Title.
PN6084.F6P65   1991
641.3—dc20   91-12415
                                                                                  CIP

Printed in the United States of America
Designed by Eve L. Kirch

For Ken

CONTENTS

ACKNOWLEDGMENTS

So many people foraged through their memories to contribute to this collection, but I would especially like to thank Bill Henderson of Pushcart Press, who gave the book its first life as *The Cook's Quotation Book*, and Meg Blackstone, who thought to expand it and give it a second life. My editor Toni Rachiele was very helpful and extraordinarily generous with her knowledge of literature and food. Genie Chipps Henderson, Craig Claiborne, Jim Charlton, Michael Disher, Pat Strachan, John Ford, Dava Sobel, Winnie Rosen, Becky Okrent, Durell Godfrey, and Andy Weil all shared their knowledge with me.

Samuel Johnson once said that man had not yet contrived anything by which so much happiness is produced as a good restaurant. I am blessed to have, right in my neighborhood, one such restaurant, and it wouldn't feel right if I didn't thank Jeff Salaway, Toni Ross, Gail Arnold, and everybody else for the addictive joy and inspiration they have afforded me.

In a category all their own are my sister Lydia and my husband Ken. Each, in a different way, is the salt of my life.

PREFACE

This book is the felicitous result of the two great and guilty pleasures of my life—eating and reading. What nostalgia I have about my childhood years has to do with the extravagant indulgence of these two happy vices. Alas, never again will there be so much time, so much leisure to curl up and read on and on, devouring books with such innocent greed. And never again either can eating be approached with such careless abandon, for now in my forties a candy bar is as rare a luxury as a pound of caviar, and buttered toast or a fried egg must be worked off in aerobic agony.

But I recall so clearly the pleasure of my first encounter with certain passages of, say, *The Wind in the Willows*. Do you remember breaking the code of "coldtonguecoldhamcoldbeef pickledgherkinssaladfrenchrollscresssandwichespotted meatgingerbeerlemonadesodawater—"? There I was feeling so clever and suddenly so hungry, and I very much agreed with Mole, who cried out in ecstasy, "Stop, stop. This is too much!" For years I carried around in my head the description, which comes later on in the same book, of a picnic basket that held a long French bread, a garlic sausage, and "some cheese which lay down and cried," so that fully a decade later when I first encountered a wedge of ripe brie,

I recognized it instantly as the very same weepy cheese. It is this connection between the literary and the culinary that I have always found irresistible.

Of course you remember the scene in *A Little Princess* where poor Sara, having gone hungry for days (even now I feel the sympathetic hunger pangs), wakes up in her garret to find a sumptuous surprise supper laid out for her. And the scene in Tom Sawyer when Huck and Tom, also hungry, as hungry as two growing boys ever were, caught some fish and fried them with bacon over a campfire for their breakfast.

And there are scenes in Dickens, and James Joyce and Trollope, and Rex Stout and Lewis Carroll and Herman Melville and Dorothy Sayers and Virginia Woolf and Colette . . . and Proust, naturally. And I could go on and on, and did for many evenings around our dinner table and the dinner tables of others, until it was decided that I should collect these culinary moments and bon mots of literature in this book.

Addendum

It's hard to believe that the slim volume introduced above appeared more than eight years ago. That's quite a long time to indulge those inevitable, delicious, and rueful second thoughts which the French call the *esprit de l'escalier*, the spirit of the staircase (the French are like that, I guess). In any case, friends exacerbated that feeling by barraging me with reminders of missed opportunities. And then I heard from readers of the original edition—hundreds of lit-

erary gastronomes (or perhaps they were gastronomic liter-
ateurs) who wrote to bemoan the omission of their favorite
quotes. All these suggestions as well as my own new discov-
eries were carefully preserved on the electronic equivalent
of 3x5 cards, though I didn't know precisely why at the
time, but literary grazing (and hoarding, too, I suppose), is
habit-forming and sometimes impossible to leave off merely
because the manuscript has gone off to the publisher.

So when Meg Blackstone, then a senior editor at Dutton,
offered to publish an expanded edition of *The Cook's Quotation Book*, I was more than ready. Of course, that hardly
means that this edition is complete or definitive. Far from
it. The bulk of literature from the past is (thankfully) too
large to exhaust in a lifetime, and new literature is added
daily—much of which just naturally must deal with the
niceties of our most basic human need, sustenance. Never-
theless, here's a new, revised, and vastly expanded Mulli-
gan stew for you. Break off a piece of bread and dip in.

M.P.R.

January 1991

A Matter of Taste

Leopold Bloom ate with relish the inner organs of beasts and fowls. He liked thick giblet soup, nutty gizzards, a stuffed roast heart, liver slices fried with breadcrumbs, fried hencod's roe. Most of all he liked grilled mutton kidneys which gave to his palate a fine tang of scented urine.

—JAMES JOYCE

In the morning, the waitress would wash down the floors of the hotel, and for that she would wear wooden clogs. At lunchtime she would take off the clogs and put on stockings and high-heeled slippers, a gesture of coquetry I can still see her performing. After she had pulled on the slippers, she would wash her hands at the spigot over a painted metal basin that was placed at the entrance of the dining room for the use of fastidious clients. She left an enduring impress on my life, although our relations were always impersonal. At my first meal at the hotel, I asked for a salad plate. She brought it to me, saying with a superior smile, "Chacun son pays, chacun sa façon." I have taken my salad on my meat plate ever since, dabbling the lettuce in the leftover gravy.   —A. J. LIEBLING

Cauliflower is nothing but cabbage with a college education.
                                                            —MARK TWAIN

Almost every person has something secret he likes to eat.
                                                            —M.F.K. FISHER

Chutney is marvelous. I'm mad about it. To me, it's very imperial.   —DIANA VREELAND

Only a Southerner knows how to fry a chicken. Period!
                                                            —ANONYMOUS

Isn't there any other part of the matzo you can eat?
                                                            —MARILYN MONROE

Miss Fisher . . . broke a croissant in two and dipped it with perfect naturalness into her coffee, smiling away at herself for some interior reason and not observing Henrietta's surprise. Henrietta was sure you did not do this to bread. . . . She sat biting precisely into her half of roll, wondering how one could bear to eat soppy bread.   —ELIZABETH BOWEN

Practically all the littleneck and cherrystone clams served on the half shell in New York restaurants come out of the black mud of Long Island bays. They are the saltiest, cleanest, and biggest-bellied clams in the world. . . .

He gave me one and we squatted on the deck and went to work opening the cherries. When the valves were pried apart, the rich clam liquor dribbled out. The flesh of the cherries was a delicate pink. On the cups of some of the shells were splotches of deep purple; Indians used to hack such splotches out of the clamshells for wampum. Fresh from the coal-black mud and uncontaminated by ketchup or sauce, they were the best clams I have ever eaten. The mate sat on the hatch and watched us.

"Aren't you going to have any?" I asked.

"I wouldn't put one of those damned things in my mouth if I was perishing to death," he said. "I'm working on this buoy-boat for ten years and I'm yet to eat a clam."

—JOSEPH MITCHELL

What is food to one may be fierce poison to others.

—LUCRETIUS

Give me a platter of choice finnan haddie, freshly cooked in its bath of water and milk, add melted butter, a slice or two of hot toast, a pot of steaming Darjeeling tea, and you may tell the butler to dispense with the caviar, truffles, and nightingales' tongues.   —CRAIG CLAIBORNE

In Mexico we have a word for sushi: bait.   —JOSÉ SIMON

Of late the cook has had the surprising sagacity to learn from the French that apples will make pyes; and it's a ques-

tion, if, in the violence of his efforts, we do not get one of apples, instead of having both of beef-steak which I prefer.
—GEORGE WASHINGTON

I might glorify my bill of fare until I was tired; but after all, the Scotchman would shake his head and say, "Where's your haggis?" and the Fijian would sigh and say, "Where's your missionary?" —MARK TWAIN

Airline Food

Do not accept any food from an airline that you would not accept from a vendor in Calcutta. If it's bottled or if you peel it yourself, it may be all right. Otherwise it may stay with you for the rest of your life. —ROY BLOUNT, JR.

Greece—Splendid little American lunches in pasteboard boxes that we ate in plane: hard-boiled eggs with salt and pepper, one beefspread sandwich, one cheese sandwich, one peanut butter and marmalade sandwich, one cookie, one small container of cut up peach and pear compote, one small bag of assorted fruit drops—with pasteboard cup for water. —EDMUND WILSON

Appetite

Appetite comes with eating. —FRANÇOIS RABELAIS

If thou rise with an Appetite, thou art sure never to sit down without one. —WILLIAM PENN

Appetite, a universal wolf. —SHAKESPEARE

He who eats for two must work for three. —KURDISH PROVERB

The poor seek food, the rich seek an appetite. —HINDI PROVERB

The appetites of the belly and the palate, far from diminishing as men grow older, go on increasing. —CICERO

He hath eaten me out of house and home. —SHAKESPEARE

'Tis not the meat, but 'tis the appetite makes eating a delight. —SIR JOHN SUCKLING

I came across excellent blackberries,—ate of them heartily. It was midday, & when I left the brambles, I found I had a sufficient meal so there was no need to go to an inn. Of a sudden it struck me as an extraordinary thing. Here had I satisfied my hunger without payment, without indebtedness to any man. The vividness with which I felt that this was extraordinary seems to me a shrewd comment on a social state which practically denies a man's right to food unless he have money. —GEORGE GISSING

Lazy fokes' stummucks don't git tired.
—JOEL CHANDLER HARRIS

Beer, Ale, and Porter

Most people hate the taste of beer—to begin with. It is, however, a prejudice that many people have been able to overcome. —WINSTON CHURCHILL

I have fed purely upon ale; I have eat my ale, drank my ale, and I always sleep upon ale. —GEORGE FARQUHAR

When I die I want to decompose in a barrel of porter and have it served in all the pubs in Dublin. I wonder would they know it was me? —J. P. DONLEAVY

Those who drink beer will think beer.
—WASHINGTON IRVING

To drink? Elephant beer, malty and mud brown, a liquid sensation that eclipses Fodor's ability to describe it.

—IRA WOOD

Berries

About the strawberry:
Doubtless God could have made a better berry, but doubtless God never did. —WILLIAM BUTLER

The Strawberry is not everyone's fruit. To some it brings a sudden rash, and to others twinges of rheumatism. This fact must be admitted and faced. —EDWARD BUNYARD

Toujours strawberries and cream. —SAMUEL JOHNSON

When I was a child, my cousins and I went on wild strawberry picking marathons. Returning from the woods, our mouths and hands would be smudged red and purple. Hardly able to stand from so much kneeling, we would beg *babushka* [grandmother] to make our favorite preserves from all our hard-won little trophies. With the seriousness of an alchemist she measured equal amounts of berries and sugar into a huge copper basin, and as the intoxicatingly sweet smelling mixture was brought to a boil, we eagerly awaited our share of the tasty foam (*penki*) that we were allowed to skim off the preserve. After that point, we lost all interest in the activity and made our way toward the prickly gooseberry bush, only to emerge an hour later all scratched and torn, but satisfied, as only eight year olds can be, with the results of our next harvest. —ANYA VON BREMZEN

Raspberries are best not washed. After all, one must have faith in something. —ANN BATCHELDER

Nobody can be insulted by raspberries and cream.
—BARBARA KAFKA

Bowl of Red

Chili lovers come from every walk of life. Chili attracts truck drivers, celebrities, doctors, lawyers, and schoolteachers. Rich and poor undergo a Jekyll/Hyde-like transformation and mild-mannered pillars of the community show no mercy when the topic of conversation turns to controversial chili.

—JANE BUTEL

The quarreling that has gone on for generations over New England clam chowder versus Manhattan clam chowder (the Maine legislature once passed a bill outlawing the mixing of tomatoes with clams) is but a minor spat alongside the raging feuds that have arisen out of chili recipes.

—MARTINA AND WILLIAM NEELY

Chili is not so much food as a state of mind. Addictions to it are formed early in life and the victims never recover. On blue days in October I get this passionate yearning for a bowl of chili, and I nearly lose my mind.

—MARGARET COUSINS

Next to jazz music, there is nothing that lifts the spirit and strengthens the soul more than a good bowl of chili.

—HARRY JAMES

The aroma of good chili should generate rapture akin to a lover's kiss. —Motto of the CHILI APPRECIATION SOCIETY INTERNATIONAL

The bowl of blessedness!
—WILL ROGERS' description of real Texas chili

Lord, God, You know us old cowhands is forgetful. Some- times, I can't even recollect what happened yestiddy. We is forgetful. We just know daylight and dark, summer, fall, winter, and spring. But we sure hope we don't never forget to thank You before we is about to eat a mess of good chili.

We don't know why, in Your wisdom, You been so dog- gone good to us. The heathen Chinee don't have no chili, ever. The Frenchmens is left out. The Rooshians don't know no more about chili than a hog does about a side saddle. Even the Meskins don't get a good whiff of it unless they stay around here.

Chili eaters is some of Your chosen people. We don't know why You so doggone good to us. But, Lord, God, don't never think we ain't grateful for this chili we about to eat. Amen. —BONES HOOKS

Chili is much improved by having had a day to contemplate its fate. —JOHN STEELE GORDON

Bread and Butter

The history of man from the beginning has been the history
of his struggle for his daily bread.   —JOSUE DE CASTRO

Here is bread, which strengthens man's heart, and therefore
is called the staff of life.   —MATTHEW HENRY

You don't get tired of muffins, but you don't find inspiration
in them.   —GEORGE BERNARD SHAW

There is good dripping toast by the fire in the evening. Good jelly dripping and crusty, home-baked bread, with the mealy savour of ripe wheat roundly in your mouth and under your teeth, roasted sweet and crisp and deep brown, and covered with little pockets where dripping will hide and melt and shine in the light, deep down inside, ready to run when your teeth bite in. Butter is good, too, mind. But I will have my butter with plain bread and butter, cut in the long slice, and I will say of its kind, there is nothing you will have better, especially if the butter is an hour out of the churn and spread tidy. —RICHARD LLEWELLYN

I do like a bit of butter to my bread. —A. A. MILNE

Honest bread is very well—it's the butter that makes the temptation. —DOUGLAS JERROLD

> And the Quangle Wangle said
> To himself on the crumpety tree
> "Jam and Jelly and bread
> are the best of foods for me."
> —EDWARD LEAR

Have you ever gone into a farmhouse kitchen on a baking day, and seen the great crock of dough set by the fire to rise? If you have, and if you were at that time still young enough to be interested in everything you saw, you will remember that you found yourself quite unable to resist the temptation to poke your finger into the soft round dough that curved inside the pan like a giant mushroom. And you will remember that your finger made a dent in the dough, and that slowly, but quite surely, the dent disappeared, and the dough looked quite the same as it did before you touched it. Unless, of course, your hand was extra dirty in which case, naturally, there would be a little black mark.

—E. NESBIT

Without bread all is misery.   —WILLIAM COBBETT

> O God! that bread should be so dear,
> And flesh and blood so cheap!
>   —THOMAS HOOD

> What hymns are sung.
> What praises said.
> For homemade miracles of bread?
>   —LOUIS UNTERMEYER

Do you know on this one block you can buy croissants in five different places? There's one store called Bonjour Croissant. It makes me want to go to Paris and open a store called Hello Toast.   —FRAN LEBOWITZ

Bread, milk and butter are of venerable antiquity. The taste of the morning of the world.   —LEIGH HUNT

Bread deals with living things, with giving life, with growth, with the seed, the grain that nurtures. It is not coincidence that we say bread is the staff of life.   —LIONEL POILANE

> "A loaf of bread," the Walrus said,
> "Is what we chiefly need:
> Pepper and vinegar besides

Are very good indeed—
Now if you're ready, Oysters dear,
We can begin to feed."
But answer there came none—
And this was scarcely odd because
They'd eaten every one.

—LEWIS CARROLL

For a few days or a week or a fortnight, the fields stood "ripe unto harvest." It was the one perfect period in the hamlet year. The human eye loves to rest upon wide expanses of pure colour: the moors in the purple heyday of the heather, miles of green downland, and the sea when it lies calm and blue and boundless, all delight it; but to some none of these, lovely though they all are, can give the same satisfaction of spirit as acres upon acres of golden corn. *There* is both beauty and bread and the seeds of bread for future generations.   —FLORA THOMPSON

Open thine eyes, and thou shalt be satisfied with bread.
                    —PROVERBS 20:13

I am going to learn to make bread to-morrow. So you may imagine me with my sleeves rolled up, mixing flour, milk, saleratus, etc., with a deal of grace. I advise you if you don't know how to make the staff of life to learn with dispatch.
                    —EMILY DICKINSON

His bread contains a thirteen-to-one ratio of unbleached flour to rye, and when it is old it is durable. It makes what he calls "good tough bread crumbs that hold up." When it is fresh, its aroma alone would melt butter. He does not make it every day because he and Anne eat so much of it they endanger their health.

—JOHN MCPHEE, on an anonymous chef

Of all smells, bread; of all tastes, salt.   —GEORGE HERBERT

In Paris today millions of pounds of bread are sold daily, made during the previous night by those strange, half-naked beings one glimpses through cellar windows, whose wild-seeming cries floating out of those depths always makes a painful impression. In the morning, one sees these pale men, still white with flour, carrying a loaf under one arm, going off to rest and gather new strength to renew their hard and useful labor when night comes again. I have always highly esteemed the brave and humble workers who labor all night to produce those soft but crusty loaves that look more like cake than bread.   —ALEXANDRE DUMAS

The smell of good bread baking, like the sound of lightly flowing water, is indescribable in its evocation of innocence and delight.   —M.F.K. FISHER

> I never had a piece of toast
> Particularly long and wide,
> But fell upon the sanded floor,
> And always on the buttered side.
>   —JAMES PAYN

Give us this day our daily bread.   —MATTHEW 6:2

I learned to bake wonderful bread—I had always thought of bread as something that just happened, but Bermuda bread was so horrible I bought some yeast and a cook book and had hot rolls for breakfast, and loaf bread for my tea.
—KATHERINE ANNE PORTER

Three little ghostesses
Sitting on postesses,
Eating buttered toastesses,
Greasing their fistesses
Up to their wristesses.
Oh, what beastesses,
To make such feastesses!
—NURSERY RHYME

Breakfast

Life, within doors, has few pleasanter prospects than a neatly arranged and well-provisioned breakfast table.
—NATHANIEL HAWTHORNE

I am one who eats breakfast gazing at morning glories.
—BASHO

To eat figs off the tree in the very early morning, when they have been barely touched by the sun, is one of the exquisite pleasures of the Mediterranean.　　—ELIZABETH DAVID

I said my prayers and ate some cranberry tart for breakfast.
—WILLIAM BYRD

The breakfast is the prosopon of the great work of the day. Chocolate, coffee, tea, cream, eggs, ham, tongue, cold fowl—all these are good and bespeak good knowledge in him who sets them forth: but the touchstone is fish: anchovy is the first step, prawns and shrimp the second; and I laud him who reaches even these: potted char and lampreys are the third . . . but lobster is, indeed, matter for a May morning and demands a rare combination of knowledge and virtue in him who sets it forth.   —THOMAS LOVE PEACOCK

What? Sunday morning in an English family and no sausages? God bless my soul, what's the world coming to, eh?
—DOROTHY SAYERS

One morning in November I awoke at 6:30 A.M. and looked out on a gray landscape that would have dispirited Gustave Doré: palpably damp, lunar in its deleafed desolation, it made my bone marrow feel as though I somehow had extracted it and left it in a dish on the back step all night. It was one of those mornings when a man could face the day only after warming himself with a mug of thick coffee beaded with steam, a good thick crust of bread, and bowl of bean soup.   —RICHARD GEHMAN

A simple enough pleasure, surely, to have breakfast alone with one's husband, but how seldom married people in the midst of life achieve it.   —ANNE MORROW LINDBERGH

My wife and I tried to breakfast together, but we had to stop or our marriage would have been wrecked.
—WINSTON CHURCHILL

The breakfast table is not a bulletin board for the curing of horrible dreams and depressing symptoms, but the place where a bright keynote for the day is struck.
—B. G. JEFFRIES

So in our pride we ordered for breakfast, an omelet, toast and coffee and what has just arrived is a tomato salad with onions, a dish of pickles, a big slice of watermelon and two bottles of cream soda.
—JOHN STEINBECK, traveling in Russia

Bring porridge, bring sausage, bring fish for a start,
Bring kidneys and mushrooms and partridges' legs,
But let the foundation be bacon and eggs.
—A. P. HERBERT

The breakfast egg was a Victorian institution (only a century old); whatever else there was for breakfast—kidneys, chops, bacon, or kedgeree, with tea or coffee, marmalade or honey—there was always a meek little cluster of boiled eggs, set modestly apart upon a chased silver stand, with their spoons beside them (like St. Ursula's virgins on shipboard).
—DOROTHY HARTLEY

The cheery noise of bubbling pancake batter was as plainly heard as the singing teakettle every morning of the year in

our house. I often lifted the cover of the batter crock to look at the bubbles, which reminded me of the eyes of animals.
—U. P. HEDRICK

Only dull people are brilliant at breakfast. —OSCAR WILDE

And now let us observe the well-furnished breakfast parlour at Plumstead Episcopi. . . . The tea consumed was the very best, the coffee the very blackest, the cream the very thickest; there was dry toast and buttered toast, muffins and crumpets; hot bread and cold bread, white bread and brown bread, home-made bread and baker's bread, wheaten bread and oaten bread; and if there be other breads than these, they were there; there were eggs in napkins, and crispy bits of bacon under silver covers; and there were little fishes in a little box, and devilled kidneys. . . . Over and above this, on a snow-white napkin . . . was a huge ham and a huge sirloin. . . . Such was the ordinary fare at Plumstead Episcopi.   —ANTHONY TROLLOPE

Breakfast is a notoriously difficult meal to serve with a flourish.   —CLEMENT FREUD

Oysters are the usual opening to a winter breakfast . . . Indeed, they are almost indispensable.
—GRIMOD DE LA REYNIÈRE

Breakfast is a forecast of the whole day: Spoil that and all is spoiled. —LEIGH HUNT

I was so darned sorry for poor old Corky that I hadn't the heart to touch my breakfast. I told Jeeves to drink it himself. —P. G. WODEHOUSE

Carnivorous Fare

Beef is the soul of cooking. —MARIE ANTOINE CARÉME

Greater eaters of meat are in general more cruel and ferocious than other men. —JEAN-JACQUES ROUSSEAU

When mighty roast beef was the Englishman's food,
It ennobled our hearts and enriched our blood,
Our soldiers were brave and our courtiers good,
Oh! The roast beef of old England!
—RICHARD LEVERIDGE

Roast Beef, Medium, is not only a food. It is a philosophy. Seated at Life's Dining Table, with the menu of Morals before you, your eye wanders a bit over the *entrées*, the hors d'oeuvres, and the things *à la* though you know that Roast Beef, Medium, is safe and sane, and sure. —EDNA FERBER

The Norman takes his vegetables in the form of animals.
"Herbivores eat grass," one hotel landlord told me. "Man,
a carnivore, eats herbivores."   —A. J. LIEBLING

I am a great eater of beef, and I believe that does harm to
my wit.   —SHAKESPEARE

Much meat, much malady.   —THOMAS FULLER

Any of us would kill a cow rather than not have beef.
                                                  —SAMUEL JOHNSON

What say you to a piece of beef and mustard?
                                                  —SHAKESPEARE

Mustard's no good without roast beef.
                    —CHICO MARX, in the movie *Monkey Business*

Though regarded with disdain by the chic, and horror by
the alfalfa-sprout crowd, hot dogs are flat-out wonderful.
And versatile. Dripping with hot onions and ball-park mustard from a Sabrett man, they taste like New York; served
in little cardboard doo-hickeys and called frankforts, they
taste like America. They also make no unreasonable demands
on the home cook.   —VLADIMIR ESTRAGON

Some hae meat and canna eat,
And some wad eat that want it;
But we hae meat, and we can eat,
And sae the Lord be thankit.

—ROBERT BURNS

Barbecue is any four-footed animal—be it mouse or
mastadon. . . . At its best it is a fat steer, and it must be
eaten within an hour of when it is cooked. For if ever the
sun rises upon Barbecue, its flavor vanishes like Cinderella's
silks. . . . staler in the chill dawn than illicit love.

—WILLIAM ALLEN WHITE

The nearer the bone the sweeter the meat.

—ENGLISH PROVERB

Give them great meals of beef and iron and steel, they will act like wolves and fight like devils. —SHAKESPEARE

Man is the only animal that can remain on friendly terms with the victims he intends to eat until he eats them.
—SAMUEL BUTLER

Veal is the quintessential Lonely Guy meat. There's something pale and lonely about it, especially if it doesn't have any veins. It's so wan and Kierkegaardian. You just know it's not going to hurt you. —BRUCE JAY FRIEDMAN

Bologna is celebrated for producing popes, painters, and sausages. —LORD BYRON

A hamburger is warm and fragrant and juicy. A hamburger is soft and nonthreatening. It personifies the Great Mother herself who has nourished us from the beginning. A hamburger is an icon of layered circles, the circle being at once the most spiritual and the most sensual of shapes. A hamburger is companionable and faintly erotic. The nipple of the Goddess, the bountiful belly-ball of Eve. You are what you think you eat. —TOM ROBBINS

And that reminds me of that wonderful little lamb stew I had the other night at Chuck Williams'—it was so wonderful you could cuddle it in your arms. —JAMES BEARD

Champagne

I'm only a beer teetotaller, not a champagne teetotaller.
—GEORGE BERNARD SHAW

I like to start off my day with a glass of champagne. I like
to wind it up with champagne, too. To be frank, I also like
a glass or two in between. It may not be the universal medicine for every disease, as my friends the champagne people
in Reims and Epernay so often tell me, but it does you less
harm than any other liquid.   —FERNAND POINT

There comes a time in every woman's life when the only
thing that helps is a glass of champagne.
—BETTE DAVIS, in the movie *Old Acquaintance*

Here's to champagne, the drink divine
That makes us forget our troubles;
It's made of a dollar's worth of wine
And three dollar's worth of bubbles.
—ANONYMOUS

Do I like champagne? Ah, no, listen, that is a very personal
question and one that I am not at liberty to answer. . . . A
less intimate question, yes. You should have asked me when

I last made love, for example. You should have asked me when I last made love and enjoyed it.
                                    —HENRI CARTIER-BRESSON, in response
                                        to a telephone survey

Come quickly, I am tasting the stars!
                                    —DOM PÉRIGNON, at the moment
                                        of his discovery of champagne

The advantage of champagne consists not only in the exhilarating sparkle and play of its mantling life, where the beads that airily rise ever in pursuit of those that have merrily passed; but in the magnetism it possesses above all other wines—of tempting the fair sex to drink an extra glass.
                                    —ST. ANGE

Champagne's funny stuff. I'm used to whiskey. Whiskey is a slap on the back, and champagne's a heavy mist before my eyes.
                —JAMES STEWART, in the movie *The Philadelphia Story*

The way I gained my title's
By a hobby which I've got
Of never letting others pay
However long the shot;
Whoever drinks at my expense
Are treated all the same,
From Dukes and Lords to cabmen down,
I make them drink Champagne.
                —ANONYMOUS MUSIC HALL SONG, 1895

Before I was born my mother was in great agony of spirit and in a tragic situation. She could take no food except iced oysters and champagne. If people ask me when I began to dance, I reply, "In my mother's womb, probably as a result of the oysters and champagne—the food of Aphrodite."
—ISADORA DUNCAN

Champagne has the taste of an apple peeled with a steel knife. —ALDOUS HUXLEY

Even for those who dislike Champagne . . . there are two Champagnes one can't refuse: Dom Perignon and the even superior Cristal, which is bottled in a natural-coloured glass

that displays its pale blaze, a chilled fire of such prickly
dryness that, swallowed, seems not to have been swallowed
at all, but instead to have been turned to vapours on the
tongue, and burned there to one sweet ash.

—TRUMAN CAPOTE

Burgundy makes you think of silly things; Bordeaux makes
you talk about them, and Champagne makes you do them.

—BRILLAT-SAVARIN

I was enjoying myself now. I had taken two finger-bowls of
Champagne, and the scene had changed before my eyes
into something significant, elemental, and profound.

—F. SCOTT FITZGERALD

A single glass of champagne imparts a feeling of exhilaration. The nerves are braced; the imagination is stirred, the
wits become more nimble.   —WINSTON CHURCHILL

Champagne and orange juice is a great drink. The orange
improves the champagne. The champagne definitely improves
the orange.   —PHILIP, DUKE OF EDINBURGH

"The bigger the better" is, though a common, not a universal rule; it does not, for instance, apply to fish, nor to
mutton. . . . But it generally applies to receptacles of wine,
and to those of champagne very specially.

—GEORGE SAINTSBURY

Cheese

Many's the long night I've dreamed of cheese—toasted, mostly.   —ROBERT LOUIS STEVENSON

Poets have been mysteriously silent on the subject of cheese.
—G. K. CHESTERTON

A cheese may disappoint. It may be dull, it may be naïve, it may be oversophisticated. Yet it remains cheese, milk's leap toward immortality.   —CLIFTON FADIMAN

Never commit yourself to a cheese without having first *examined* it.   —T. S. ELIOT

An apple-pie without some cheese
Is like a kiss without a squeeze.   —ANONYMOUS

People who know nothing about cheeses reel away from Camembert, Roquefort and Stilton because the plebeian proboscis is not equipped to differentiate between the sordid and the sublime.   —HARVEY DAY

Processed "cheese." The word should always, like Soviet "democracy," be framed in quotes, for no matter what the law may say, I refuse to call this cheese. . . . The best I can say for it is that it is not poisonous; the worst, that it represents the triumph of technology over conscience.

In the preparation of this solidified floor wax . . . every problem but one is solved: packaging, keeping, distribution, slicing, cost. One problem alone is not solved: that of making cheese.   —BOB BROWN

Cheese is probably the friendliest of foods. It endears itself to everything and never tires of showing off to great advantage. Any liquor or, I may say, any potable or any edible loves to be seen in the company of cheese. Naturally, some nationalities choose one type of companion and some another, but you very seldom find clashes of temperament in passing.   —JAMES BEARD

The great Norman cheeses were served as well: Camembert, Pont l'Évêque, and the stinky Livarot. But my father warned: "Not for Mademoiselle Simone, the strong cheeses." He thought young girls shouldn't be allowed to pollute their mouths with smelly odors.   —SIMONE BECK

Chic Food

Summer has an unfortunate effect upon hostesses who have been unduly influenced by the photography of Irving Penn and take the season as a cue to serve dinners of astonishingly meager proportions. These they call light, a quality which, while most assuredly welcome in comedies, cotton shirts and hearts, is not an appropriate touch at dinner.

—FRAN LEBOWITZ

Chicken salad has a certain glamour about it. Like the little black dress, it is chic and adaptable anywhere.

—LAURIE COLWIN

Strawberries, and only strawberries, could now be thought or spoken of. "The best fruit in England—everybody's favourite—always wholesome. These the finest beds and finest sorts. Delightful to gather for oneself—the only way of really enjoying them. Morning decidedly the best time—never tired—every sort good—hautboy infinitely superior—no comparison—the others hardly eatable—hautboys very scarce—Chili preferred—white wood finest flavour of all—price of strawberries in London . . . only objection to gathering strawberries the stooping—glaring sun—tired to death—could bear it no longer—must go and sit in the shade." Such, for half an hour, was the conversation.

—JANE AUSTEN

For everyone doing rustic food, there are others out there braiding chives.   —JOYCE GOLDSTEIN

Mmmmmmmmmmmmmmmmmm. These are nice. Little Roquefort cheese morsels rolled in crushed nuts. Very tasty. Very subtle. It's the way the dry sackiness of the nuts tiptoes up against the dour savour of the cheese that is so nice, so subtle. Wonder what the Black Panthers eat here on the hors-d'oeuvre trail? Do the Panthers like little Roquefort cheese morsels rolled in crushed nuts this way, and asparagus tips in mayonnaise dabs, and meatballs petites au Coq Hardi, all of which are at the very moment being offered to them on gadrooned silver platters by maids in black uniforms with hand-ironed white aprons. —TOM WOLFE

Lettuce is divine, although I'm not sure it's really a food.
—DIANA VREELAND

Chicken and Other Birds

I want there to be no peasant in my kingdom so poor that he is unable to have a chicken in his pot on Sundays.
—HENRI IV OF FRANCE

A chicken in every pot.
—HERBERT HOOVER

Gorbachev has a new slogan: A chicken in every time zone.
—JOHNNY CARSON

Poultry is for the cook what canvas is for the painter.
—BRILLAT-SAVARIN

What is sauce for the goose may be sauce for the gander, but it is not necessarily sauce for the chicken, the duck, the turkey or the Guinea hen.
—ALICE B. TOKLAS

Turkey boiled is turkey spoiled
And turkey roast is turkey lost
But for turkey braise
The Lord be praised.

—ANONYMOUS

No more turkey, but I'd like another helping of that bread he ate.

—ANONYMOUS, quoted in *Joy of Cooking*

You first parents of the human race . . . who ruined yourself for an apple, what might you not have done for a truffled turkey? —BRILLAT-SAVARIN

When I demanded of my friend what viands he preferred,
He quoth: "A large cold bottle, and a small hot bird!"

—EUGENE FIELD

A goose is a silly bird, too much for one, not enough for two. —POOLE

We didn't starve, but we didn't eat chicken unless we were sick, or the chicken was. —BERNARD MALAMUD

It is to be regretted that domestication has seriously deteriorated the moral character of the duck. In a wild state, he is a faithful husband . . . but no sooner is he domesticated than he becomes polygamous, and makes nothing of owning ten or a dozen wives at a time.

—MRS. ISABELLA BEETON

The Cocktail Party

Of all so-called entertainment the cocktail party, it seems to me, has least to be said for it. Nasty sticky little drinks taken standing, no proper conversation, nothing worth while to eat. Anyone that one does want to speak to is immediately seized away by somebody else—I'd much rather stay home and write to you. —RUPERT HART-DAVIS

If you happen to be unencumbered by childhood's scruples and maturity's sage ponderings, you will have gone to a great many cocktail parties in your time and will have decided, along with almost every other thing human left alive, that they are anathema. They are expensive. They are dull. They are good for a time, like a dry Martini, and like that all-demanding drink they can lift you high and then drop you hideously into a slough of boredom, morbidity, and indigestion. —M.F.K. FISHER

I have very poor and unhappy brains for drinking: I could well wish courtesy would invent some other custom of entertainment. —SHAKESPEARE

A toast to the Cocktail Party
Where olives are speared
And friends are stabbed.
—ANONYMOUS

The cocktail party is a form of friendship without warmth and devotion. It is a device either for getting rid of social obligations hurriedly en masse, or for making overtures towards more serious relationships, as in the etiquette of whoring.   —BROOKS ATKINSON

> The cocktail is a pleasant drink;
> It's mild and harmless I don't think,
> When you've had one you call for two,
> And then you don't care what you do.
>   —GEORGE ADE

Who hath woe? Who hath sorrow? Who hath contentions? Who hath babbling? Who hath wounds without cause? Who hath redness of eyes? They that tarry long at the wine; they that go to seek mixed wine.   —PROVERBS 13:29–30

Coffee

> Coffee:
> Black as the devil,
> Hot as hell,
> Pure as an angel,
> Sweet as love.
> —CHARLES MAURICE DE TALLEYRAND-PÉRIGORD

If this is coffee, please bring me some tea; if this is tea, please bring me some coffee.

—ABRAHAM LINCOLN

The morning cup of coffee has an exhilaration about it which the cheering influence of the afternoon or evening cup of tea cannot be expected to reproduce.

—OLIVER WENDELL HOLMES, SR.

A cup of coffee—real coffee—home-browned, home-ground, home made, that comes to you dark as a hazel-eye, but changes to a golden bronze as you temper it with cream that never cheated, but was real cream from its birth, thick, tenderly yellow, perfectly sweet, neither lumpy nor frothing on the Java: such a cup of coffee is a match for twenty blue devils and will exorcise them all.   —HENRY WARD BEECHER

Coffee should be black as Hell, strong as death, and sweet as love.   —TURKISH PROVERB

Coffee: Induces wit. Good only if it comes through Havre. After a big dinner party it is taken standing up. Take it without sugar—very swank: gives the impression you have lived in the East.   —GUSTAVE FLAUBERT

Coffee is a fleeting moment and a fragrance.

—CLAUDIA RODEN

Among the numerous luxuries of the table, unknown to our forefathers, coffee may be considered as one of the most valuable. Its taste is very agreeable, and its flavour uncommonly so; but its principle excellence depends on its salubrity, and on its exhilarating quality. It excites cheerfulness, without intoxication; and the pleasing flow of spirits which it occasions . . . is never followed by sadness, languor or debility. It diffuses over the whole frame a glow of health, and sense of ease and well-being which is extremely delightful: existence is felt to be a positive enjoyment, and the mental powers are awakened and rendered uncommonly active.

—BENJAMIN THOMPSON

The best maxim I know in life, is to drink your coffee when you can, and when you cannot, to be easy without it.

—JONATHAN SWIFT

A cup of coffee detracts nothing from your intellect; on the contrary your stomach is freed by it and no longer distresses your brain; it will not hamper your mind with troubles but give freedom to its working. Suave molecules of Mocha stir up your blood without causing excessive heat; the organ of thought receives from it a feeling of sympathy; work becomes easier and you will sit down without distress to your principal repast which will restore your body and afford you a calm delicious night.

—CHARLES MAURICE DE TALLEYRAND-PÉRIGORD

Comfort and Consolation

Never you tell, but I'll make her a pudding, a pudding she'll like, too, and I'll pay for it myself; so mind you see she eats it. Many a one has been comforted in their sorrow by seeing a good dish come upon the table. —E. S. GASKELL

Imagine, if you can, what the rest of the evening was like. How they crouched by the fire which blazed and leaped and made much of itself in the little grate. How they removed the covers of the dishes, and found rich, hot savory soup, which was a meal in itself, and sandwiches and toast and muffins enough for both of them.

—FRANCES HODGSON BURNETT

In moments of considerable strain I tend to take to bread-and-butter pudding. There is something about the blandness of soggy bread, the crispness of the golden outer crust and the unadulterated pleasure of a lightly set custard that makes the world seem a better place to live.

—CLEMENT FREUD

There is nothing better on a cold wintry day than a properly made pot pie. —CRAIG CLAIBORNE

As I drove in she was walking into the house with eggs for breakfast and homemade biscuits ready for baking. Somehow in rural Southern culture, food is always the first thought of neighbors when there is trouble. That is something they can do and not feel uncomfortable. It is something they do not have to explain or discuss or feel self-conscious about. "Here I brought you some fresh eggs for your breakfast. And here's a cake. And some potato salad." It means, "I love you. And I am sorry for what you are going through and I will share as much of your burden as I can." And maybe potato salad is a better way of saying it.

—WILL D. CAMPBELL

After many banquets, then you have comforting *congee* with salty pickles—one mouthful *congee*, one little mouthful of salt pickle, just like tea and toast to you. If there is sickness, some chicken goes in, but there should be no fat in comforting food because it sits badly in the stomach.

—FLORENCE LIN

What comforted me? That is easy. It was a strong cold chicken jelly so very, very thick. My Mother's Chinese cook would fix it. He would cook it down, condense it—this broth with all sorts of feet in it, then it would gell into sheer bliss. It kept me alive once for three weeks when I was ill as a child. And I've always craved it since.   —JAMES BEARD

The smell of buttered toast simply talked to Toad, and with no uncertain voice; talked of warm kitchens, of breakfasts on bright frosty mornings, of cosy parlour firesides on winter evenings, when one's ramble was over and slippered feet were propped on the fender; of the purring of contented cats, and the twitter of sleepy canaries.

—KENNETH GRAHAME

Gazing at the typewriter in moments of desperation, I console myself with three thoughts: alcohol at six, dinner at eight and to be immortal you've got to be dead.

—GYLES BRANDETH

O poor immortal comforts: fish, some bread and wine.

—NIKOS KAZANTZAKIS

Company for Dinner

Because he was dining alone, his cook assumed a simple meal would do but his error was quickly corrected when Lucullus responded, "What? Did you not know, then, that today Lucullus dines with Lucullus?"   —PLUTARCH

> I write these precepts for immortal Greece,
> That round a table delicately spread,
> Or three, or four, may sit in choice repast,
> Or five at most. Who otherwise shall dine,
> Are like a troop marauding for their prey.
>
> —ARCHESTRATUS

I feel now that gastronomical perfection can be reached in these combinations: one person dining alone, usually upon a couch or hillside; two people of no matter what sex or age, dining in a good restaurant; six people, of no matter what sex or age, dining in a good home. —M.F.K. FISHER

A man should not so much respect what he eateth as with whom he eateth. —MICHEL DE MONTAIGNE

> Heavenly Father, bless us,
> And keep us all alive,
> There's ten of us to dinner
> And not enough for five.
>
> —ANONYMOUS

Oh, the pleasure of eating my dinner alone!
—CHARLES LAMB

We should look for someone to eat and drink with before looking for something to eat and drink, for dining alone is leading the life of a lion or wolf. —EPICURUS

You'll never get a good party going without giving things a bit of a push. It boils down to the same formula most times: good setting, good food, good drink and plenty of goodwill, as is right at this time of the year. —MICHAEL SMITH

The more the merrier; the fewer, the better fare.
—JOHN PALSGRAVE

Compulsive Behavior

If one begins eating peanuts one cannot stop.
—H. L. MENCKEN AND GEORGE JEAN NATHAN

I hate television. I hate it as much as peanuts. But I can't
stop eating peanuts. —ORSON WELLES

Statistics show that of those who contract the habit of eating,
very few ever survive. —WILLIAM WALLACE IRWIN

Condiments, Herbs, and Spices

Black pepper heate and comfort the brain. —JOHN GERARD

Parsley—the jewel of herbs, both in the pot and on the
plate. —ALBERT STOCKLI

Mayonnaise: One of the sauces which serve the French in
place of a state religion. —AMBROSE BIERCE

On béarnaise sauce:

It frightens me! With it one might never stop eating. Merely reading the recipe arouses my hunger.   —BARON BRISSE

Mustard: Good only in Dijon. Ruins the stomach.
                                                —GUSTAVE FLAUBERT

Pepper is small in quantity and great in virtue.   —PLATO

A man who is stingy with saffron is capable of seducing his own grandmother.   —NORMAN DOUGLAS

In medieval times the habit arose of expressing a man's wealth, no longer in terms of the amount of land in his estate, but of the amount of pepper in his pantry. One way of saying that a man was poor was to say that he lacked pepper. The wealthy kept large stores of pepper in their houses, and let it be known that it was there: it was a guarantee of solvency.   —WAVERLEY ROOT

Vinegar, the son of wine.   —HEBREW PROVERB

Consider the Oyster

A beatific smile spread over his face!
  Man had tasted the oyster!
  In half an hour, mankind was plunging into the waves

searching for oysters. The oyster's doom was sealed. His monstrous pretension that he belonged in the van of evolutionary progress was killed forever. He had been tasted, and found food. He would never again battle for supremacy. Meekly he yielded to his fate. He is food to this day.

—DON MARQUIS

Oysters are not really food, but are relished to bully the sated stomach into further eating. —SENECA

He was a very valiant man who first adventured on eating oysters. —THOMAS FULLER

I will not eat oysters. I want my food dead—not sick, not wounded—dead. —WOODY ALLEN

"But wait a bit," the Oysters cried,
"Before we have our chat.
For some of us are out of breath,
And all of us are fat!"

—LEWIS CARROLL

Oysters are more beautiful than any religion. . . . There's nothing in Christianity or Buddhism that quite matches the sympathetic unselfishness of an oyster. —SAKI

Actually in our present conditions of life the thing without price would seem to be more the oyster, if it were a good one, than the pearl, the quality of fake jewelry having risen in exactly inverse proportion to that of real seafood.

—ELEANOR CLARK

Oysters: Nobody eats them anymore; too expensive.

—GUSTAVE FLAUBERT

An oyster, that marvel of delicacy, that concentration of sapid excellence, that mouthful before all other mouthfuls, who first had faith to believe it, and courage to execute? The exterior is not persuasive.   —HENRY WARD BEECHER

He had often eaten oysters, but had never had enough.

—W. S. GILBERT

The Oyster—the mere writing of the word creates sensations of succulence—gastronomical pleasures, nutritive fare, easy digestion, palatable indulgence—then go to sleep in peace.   —"LUCULLUS" (1878)

I never was much of an oyster eater, nor can I relish them IN NATURALIBUS as some do, but require a quantity of sauces, lemons, cayenne peppers, bread and butter, and so forth, to render them palatable.   —WILLIAM M. THACKERAY

Oyster dear to the gourmet, beneficent Oyster, exciting rather than sating, all stomachs digest you, all stomachs bless you.   —SENECA

You have never seen the sea, but in an oyster on the shell.

—EDMOND ROSTAND

Beneficent Oyster, good to taste, good for the stomach and the soul, grant us the blessing of your further mystery.

—ELEANOR CLARK

Cooks and the Art of Cooking

Noncooks think it's silly to invest two hours' work in two minutes' enjoyment; but if cooking is evanescent, well, so is the ballet.　　　　　　　　　　　　　—JULIA CHILD

Once learnt, this business of cooking was to prove an ever growing burden. It scarcely bears thinking about, the time and labour that man and womankind has devoted to the preparation of dishes that are to melt and vanish in a moment like smoke or a dream, like a shadow, and as a post that hastes by, and the air closes behind them, afterwards no sign where they went is to be found.

—ROSE MACAULAY

If you throw a lamb chop in the oven, what's to keep it from getting done?

—JOAN CRAWFORD, in the movie *The Women*

Cooking is like love. It should be entered into with abandon or not at all. —HARRIET VAN HORNE

Woe to the cook whose sauce has no sting. —CHAUCER

Cookery is become an art, a noble science; cooks are gentlemen. —ROBERT BURTON

He makes his cook his merit, and the world visits his dinner and not him. —MOLIÈRE

Plain cooking cannot be entrusted to plain cooks. —COUNTESS MORPHY

No artist can work simply for results; he must also *like* the work of getting them. Not that there isn't a lot of drudgery in any art—and more in cooking than in most—but that if a man has never been pleasantly surprised at the way the custard sets or flour thickens, there is not much hope of making a cook of him. —ROBERT FARRAR CAPON

The art of cookery is the art of poisoning mankind, by rendering the appetite still importunate, when the wants of nature are supplied. —FRANCOIS DE SALIGNAC DE LA MOTHE FENELON

Heaven sends us good meat, but the devil sends cooks. —DAVID GARRICK

My mother was a good recreational cook, but what she basically believed about cooking was that if you worked hard and prospered, someone else would do it for you.

—NORA EPHRON

One glance at her and I knew at once the sort of things that Dorcas would cook, that Dorcas was born to cook. Never, in later life, have I sat down to dinner without saying to myself, "Ah! things look Dorcassy tonight!" or, "Alas! there is nothing Dorcassy here."

—DON MARQUIS

And please don't cook me, kind sirs! I am a good cook myself, and cook better than I cook, if you see what I mean. I'll cook beautifully for you, a perfectly beautiful breakfast for you, if only you won't have me for supper.

—BILBO BAGGINS, to the
Trolls in J.R.R. Tolkien's
The Hobbit

Like most fine cooks, M. Buillon flew into rages and wept easily; the heat of kitchens perhaps affects cooks' tear ducts as well as their tempers.

—A. J. LIEBLING

Did it matter, did it matter in the least, one Prime Minister
more, or less? It made no difference at this hour of the night
to Mrs. Walker among the plates, saucepans, cullenders,
frying-pans, chickens in aspic, ice-cream freezers, pared
crusts of bread, lemons, soup tureens, and pudding basins
which, however hard they washed up in the scullery
seemed to be all on top of her, on the kitchen table, on
chairs, while the fire blared and roared, the electric lights
glared, and still supper had to be laid. All she felt was, one
Prime Minister more or less made not a scrap of difference
to Mrs. Walker.   —VIRGINIA WOOLF

At the root of many a woman's failure to become a great
cook lies her failure to develop a workmanlike regard for
knives.   —ROBERT FARRAR CAPON

She died with a knife in her hand in her kitchen, where she
had cooked for fifty years, and her death was solemnly
listed in the newspaper as that of an artist.
                    —JANET FLANNER (GENÉT) writing about the death
                        of Mother Soret of Lyons, whose "chicken in
                        half mourning" was famous all over France

Too many cooks spoil the broth.   —ENGLISH PROVERB

Too many cooks spoil the brothel.   —POLLY ADLER

What I love about cooking is that after a hard day, there is
something comforting about the fact that if you melt butter
and add flour and then hot stock, *it will get thick!* It's a sure
thing! It's a sure thing in a world where nothing is sure; it

has a mathematical certainty in a world where those of us who long for some kind of certainty are forced to settle for crossword puzzles. —NORA EPHRON

The fricassee with dumplings is made by a Mrs. Miller whose husband has left her four times on account of her disposition and returned four times on account of her cooking and is still there. —REX STOUT

The cook was a good cook, as cooks go; and as cooks go she went. —SAKI

All of my experience in the kitchen has taught me that survival depends on letting someone else do the cooking. —ISRAEL SHENKER

When men reach their sixties and retire, they go to pieces. Women go right on cooking. —GAIL SHEEHY

I had never touched a raw chicken and it filled me with horror. —IRENE MAYER SELZNICK

Men cook more, and we all know why. It is the only interesting household task. Getting down and scrubbing the floor is done by women, or by the women they've hired. —NORA EPHRON

If you are lazy and dump everything together, they won't come out as well as if you add one thing at a time. It's like everything else; no shortcuts without compromising quality. —LIONEL POILANE

The French approach to food is characteristic; they bring to their consideration of the table the same appreciation, respect, intelligence and lively interest that they have for the other arts, for painting, for literature, and for the theatre. We foreigners living in France respect and appreciate this point of view but deplore their too strict observance of a tradition which will not admit the lightest deviation in a seasoning or the suppression of a single ingredient. Restrictions aroused our American ingenuity, we found combinations and replacements which pointed in new directions and created a fresh and absorbing interest in everything pertaining to the kitchen. —ALICE B. TOKLAS

No mean woman can cook well, for it calls for a light head, a generous spirit, and a large heart. —PAUL GAUGUIN

They were talking in the kitchen, where Catherine had started to prepare a *risotto* with whatever remains she could find. She was mincing some cold meat in her mincing machine, which was called "Beatrice," a strangely gentle and gracious name for the fierce little iron contraption whose strong teeth so ruthlessly pounded up meat and gristle. It always reminded Catherine of an African god with its square head and little short arms, and it was not at all unlike some of the crudely carved images with evil expressions and aggressively pointed breasts which Tom had brought back from Africa. —BARBARA PYM

The greatest animal in creation, the animal who cooks. —DOUGLAS JERROLD

Kissing don't last: cookery do.   —GEORGE MEREDITH

I have always thought geniuses much inferior to the plain
sense of the cookmaid, who can make a good pudding and
keep the kitchen in order.   —MARY WORTLEY MONTAGU

I seem to you cruel and too much addicted to gluttony,
when I beat my cook for sending up a bad dinner. If that
seems to you too trifling a cause, pray tell for what cause
you would have a cook flogged.   —MARTIAL

I like a cook who smiles out loud when he tastes his own
work. Let God worry about your modesty; I want to see
your enthusiasm.   —ROBERT FARRAR CAPON

The secret to good cooking resides in the cook's ability to
say "the hell with the basic recipe" and improvise freely
from it. If you haven't got this kind of moxie, you might as
well hang up your apron.   —JAMES ALAN MCPHERSON

Routine in cuisine is a crime.   —ÉDOUARD NIGNON

> They had a cook with them who stood alone
> For boiling chicken with a marrow-bone,
> Sharp flavouring powder and a spice for savour.
> He could distinguish London ale by flavour,
> And he could roast and boil and seethe and fry,
> Make good thick soup and bake a tasty pie . . .
> As for blancmange, he made it with the best.
>   —CHAUCER

Bad cooks—and the utter lack of reason in the kitchen—
have delayed human development longest and impaired it
most.   —FRIEDRICH NIETZSCHE

> To cookery we owe well-ordered States
> Assembling man in dear society
> . . . The art of cookery drew us gently forth
> From that ferocious life when, void of faith,
> The Anthropophagian ate his brother.
>
> —HESIOD

Recipes are like poems; they keep what kept us. And good
cooks are like poets; they know how to count.
                                      —HENRI COULETTE

Good cooking does not depend on whether the dish is large
or small, expensive or economical. If one has the art, then
a piece of celery or salted cabbage can be made into a mar-
vellous delicacy; whereas if one has not the art, not all the
greatest delicacies and rarities of land, sea or sky are of any
avail.   —YUAN MEI

Some people's food always tastes better than others, even
if they are cooking the same dish at the same dinner. Now
I will tell you why—because one person has more life in
them—more fire, more vitality, more guts—than others. A
person without these things can never make food taste right,
no matter what materials you give them, it is no use. Turn
in the whole cow full of cream instead of milk, and all the
fresh butter and ingredients in the world, and still that cooking will taste dull and flabby—just because they have noth-

ing in themselves to give. You have got to throw feeling into cooking. —ROSA LEWIS

The true cook is the perfect blend, the only perfect blend, of artist and philosopher. He knows his worth: he holds in his palm the happiness of mankind, the welfare of generations yet unborn. —NORMAN DOUGLAS

It is the sauce that distinguishes a good chef. The *saucier* is a soloist in the orchestra of a great kitchen.
—FERNAND POINT

M. Bourgignon, our "chef saucier," told me that by the time a chef is forty he is either dead or crazy. —DAVID OGILVY

Cooking in all its branches should be studied as a science, and not be looked upon as a haphazard mode of getting through life. —LAFCADIO HEARN

I know that there are people who say that raw materials of the highest order are the key to a good meal. I agree that a perfect peach is a fine thing, and I say also that the decline of the tomato in these United States vitiates the quality of what we eat beyond the rescue of a mere cook's ingenuity. But there is another side (at least one) to this question. A cook can make a difference. A custard is more than the sum of its yolk and sugar parts. The play of the culinary intellect yields a palatable profit on the plate. And it is nonsense to say that complex results are not just as tasty and more *interesting* than simple ones. A sauce, in other words, adds something, really two things: a taste as well as the opportunity to think about how the thing was made. This is the same kind of pleasure we derive when we look at a painting; the eye is pleased, while the mind explores the esthetic windings of a technique and a willed structure.

—RAYMOND SOKOLOV

A master cook! why he's the man of men,
For a professor; he designs, he draws,
He paints, he carves, he builds, he fortifies,
Makes citadels of curious fowl and fish.
Some he dry-ditches, some moats round with broths,
Mounts marrow-bones, cuts fifty angled custards,
Rears bulwark pies; and for his outer works,
He raiseth ramparts of immortal crust,
And teacheth all the tactics at one dinner—
What ranks, what files to put his dishes in,
The whole art military!   —BEN JONSON

In cooking, as in all the arts, simplicity is the sign of perfection.   —CURNONSKY

Successful cooks do as little as possible to achieve whatever desired results.   —ALAN KOEHLER

Cuisine is when things taste like themselves.

—CURNONSKY

Country Life

"Country life has its conveniences," he would sometimes say. "You sit on the veranda and drink tea, while your ducks swim on the pond, there is a delicious smell everywhere . . . and the gooseberries are growing."
—ANTON CHEKHOV

Life is a difficult thing in the country and it requires a good deal of forethought to steer the ship, when you live twelve miles from a lemon.　　　　　　　—SYDNEY SMITH

Cucumber

A cucumber should be well sliced, and dressed with pepper and vinegar, and then thrown out, as good for nothing.
—SAMUEL JOHNSON

"It is an art all too seldom met with," Adam declared, "the correct slicing of cucumber. In Victorian times there was—I believe—an implement or device for the purpose."
—BARBARA PYM

Curry

This curry was like a performance of Beethoven's Ninth Symphony that I'd once heard played on a player and amplifier built by personnel of the Royal Electrical and Mechanical Engineers, especially the last movement, with everything screaming and banging "Joy." It stunned, it made one fear great art. My father could say nothing after the meal.

—ANTHONY BURGESS

In the beginning there was James Beard and there was curry and that was about all. —NORA EPHRON

Danger Lurks

Zee always went naked in the house, except for the brassiere she wore when it was her turn to get dinner. Once, cooking French-fried potatoes in a kettle of boiling fat, she had come within an inch of crisping her most striking features.

—G. S. Albee

For unknown foods, the nose acts always as a sentinel and cries, Who goes there?　　　　　　　—Brillat-Savarin

Gourmets dig their graves with their teeth.

—French proverb

Some people are alarmed if the company are thirteen in number. The number is only to be dreaded when the dinner is provided but for twelve.　　　　—Lancelot Sturgeon

Eating should be done in silence, lest the windpipe open before the gullet, and life be in danger.   —THE TALMUD

In Japan, chefs offer the flesh of the puffer fish, or *fugu*, which is highly poisonous unless prepared with exquisite care. The most distinguished chefs leave just enough of the poison in the flesh to make the diners' lips tingle, so that they know how close they are to coming to their mortality. Sometimes, of course, a diner comes too close, and each year a certain number of *fugu*-lovers die in midmeal.

—DIANE ACKERMAN

Durian and Brazil Nut. An odd pair? Yes, but they have this in common, that you have to be careful they don't drop on your head.   —ALAN DAVIDSON

No Roman was ever able to say, "I dined last night with the Borgias."   —MAX BEERBOHM

Digestion and Indigestion

Peter was ill during the evening, on consequence of overeating himself. His mother put him to bed and gave him a dose of camomile tea, but Flopsy, Mopsy and Cottontail had bread and milk and blackberries for supper.

—BEATRIX POTTER

The receipts of cookery are swelled to a volume; but a good stomach excels them all.   —WILLIAM PENN

To eat is human; to digest, divine.
                                            —CHARLES T. COPELAND

Indigestion: A disease which the patient and his friends frequently mistake for deep religious conviction and concern for the salvation of mankind. As the simple Red Man of the Western Wild put it, with, it must be confessed, a certain force: "Plenty well, no pray; big belly ache, heap God."
                                            —AMBROSE BIERCE

Indigestion is charged by God with enforcing morality on the stomach.   —VICTOR HUGO

Digestion: The conversion of victuals into virtues.
                                            —AMBROSE BIERCE

Part of the secret of success in life is to eat what you like and let the food fight it out inside.   —MARK TWAIN

Nature will castigate those who don't masticate.
                                            —HORACE FLETCHER

The cold truth is that family dinners are more often than not an ordeal of nervous indigestion, preceded by hidden resentment and ennui and accompanied by psychosomatic jitters.   —M.F.K. FISHER

Oh! I ate them all
And oh! What a stomachache—
Green stolen apples!

—SHIKI

Sir Osbert once recalled that while he was attending Eton a classmate committed suicide. At the memorial service, the headmaster asked the boys whether they could give any hint as to why so well-liked and highly regarded a lad should have done away with himself. A moment of silence. Then the proverbial boy in the back timidly waved his hand: "Do you suppose, sir, it might have been the food?"

—WILLARD R. ESPY

There is no question that Rumanian-Jewish food is heavy. One meal is equal in heaviness, I would guess, to eight or nine years of steady mung-bean eating. Following the Rumanian tradition, garlic is used in excess to keep the vampires away; following the Jewish tradition, a dispenser of schmaltz (liquid chicken fat) is kept on the table to give the vampires heartburn if they get through the garlic defense.

—CALVIN TRILLIN

Roumanian-Yiddish cooking has killed more Jews than Hitler.   —ZERO MOSTEL

The only way to keep your health is to eat what you don't want, drink what you don't like, and do what you'd rather not.   —MARK TWAIN

Health food makes me sick.   —CALVIN TRILLIN

> My soul is dark with stormy riot,
> Directly traceable to diet.
> > —SAMUEL HOFFENSTEIN

The stomach . . . is a very hospitable gentleman, who is unfashionable enough to live in a sunk storey, as his ancestors have always done before him since the memory of man. The palate is the footman, whose duty it is to receive all strangers at the top of the stairs, and to announce their rank and quality before they are suffered to descend to the apartments of his master. The latter is occasionally rather irritable and choleric, and in such humours, scruples not to kick out his guests, when their company is disagreeable, who rush past the astonished footman at the landing-place and make their exit with far less ceremony and precipitation.
                                              —ANONYMOUS

Unquiet meals make ill digestions.   —SHAKESPEARE

Dinners and the Art of Dining

When my mother had to get dinner for eight she'd just make enough for sixteen and only serve half.
                                              —GRACIE ALLEN

I do not think that anything serious should be done after dinner, as nothing should be before breakfast.

—GEORGE SAINTSBURY

Music with dinner is an insult both to the cook and the violinist. —G. K. CHESTERTON

Everything depended upon things being served up the precise moment they were ready. The beef, the bay leaf, and the wine—all must be done to a turn. To keep it waiting was out of the question. Yet of course tonight, of all nights, out they went, and they came in late, and things had to be kept hot; the Boeuf en Daube would be entirely spoilt.

—VIRGINIA WOOLF

During the whole repast, the general conversation was upon eating. Every dish was discussed, and the antiquities of every bottle of wine supplied with the most eloquent annotations. Talleyrand himself analyzed the dinner with as much interest and seriousness as if he had been discussing some political question of importance.

—FRANCES, LADY SHELLEY

Dinner at the Huntercombe's possessed only two dramatic features—the wine was a farce and the food a tragedy.

—ANTHONY POWELL

If you accept a dinner invitation—you have a moral obligation to be amusing.

—DUCHESS OF WINDSOR (Wallis Simpson)

At a dinner party one should eat wisely but not too well, and talk well but not too wisely.
—W. SOMERSET MAUGHAM

A man who can dominate a London dinner table can dominate the world. —OSCAR WILDE

Dining is and always was a great artistic opportunity.
—FRANK LLOYD WRIGHT

One cannot think well, love well, sleep well, if one has not dined well. —VIRGINIA WOOLF

There is a universe between the meal set brusquely before you and that on which thought and careful planning have been spent. —EDWARD BUNYARD

The Wordsworths never dine . . . they hate such doings; when they are hungry they go to the cupboard and eat . . . Mr. Wordsworth will live for a whole month on cold beef, and next on cold bacon. —MRS. HOLLAND, in a letter

Towards freshness and presumption he was unmerciful. . . . There was a lady once who ventured an impertinence. Sitting next to Trollope at dinner she noticed that he partook largely of every dish offered to him. "You seem to have a very good appetite, Mr. Trollope," she observed. "None at all, Madam," he replied, "but thank God, I am very greedy." —MICHAEL SADLER

It is not greedy to enjoy a good dinner, any more than it is greedy to enjoy a good concert. But I do think there is something greedy about trying to enjoy the concert and dinner at the same time. —G. K. CHESTERTON

Americans are just beginning to regard food the way the French always have. Dinner is not what you do in the evening before something else. Dinner is the evening.
—ART BUCHWALD

Sir, respect your dinner: idolize it, enjoy it properly. You will be many hours in the week, many weeks in the year, and many years in your life happier if you do.
—WILLIAM M. THACKERAY

> All people are made alike.
> They are made of bones, flesh and dinners.
> Only the dinners are different.
> —GERTRUDE LOUISE CHENEY

After a good dinner, one can forgive anybody, even one's own relations. —OSCAR WILDE

Dining is the privilege of civilisation. . . . The nation which knows how to dine has learnt the leading lesson of progress. It implies both the will and the skill to reduce to order, and surround with idealisms and graces, the more material conditions of human existence; and wherever that will and that skill exist, life cannot be wholly ignoble.
—MRS. ISABELLA BEETON

Eating Outdoors

There is a charm in improvised eating which a regular meal lacks, and there was a glamour never to be recaptured in secret picnics on long sunny mornings on the roof of the Hall. . . . I would sit up there with my cousin Tooter, consuming sweets bought with our weekly pocket money and discussing possible futures. . . . The sweets I remember best were white and tubular, much thinner than any cigarette, filled with a dark chocolate filling. If I found one now I am sure it would have the taste of hope.   —GRAHAM GREENE

Give me books, fruit, French wine, fine weather and a little music out of doors, played by somebody I do not know.
—JOHN KEATS

They fried the fish with bacon and were astonished; for no fish had ever seemed so delicious before. They did not know that the quicker a fresh water fish is on the fire after he is caught the better he is; and they reflected little upon what a sauce, open air sleeping, open air exercise, bathing, and a large ingredient of hunger makes, too.   —MARK TWAIN

The wonderful world of home appliances now makes it possible to cook indoors with charcoal and outdoors with gas.
—BILL VAUGHAN

On a sheep-cropped knoll under a clump of elms we ate the strawberries and drank the wine—as Sebastian promised, they were delicious together—and we lit fat, Turkish cigarettes and lay on our backs, Sebastian's eyes on the leaves above him, mine on his profile, while the blue-grey smoke rose, untroubled by any wind, to the blue-green shadows of foliage, and the sweet scent of the tobacco merged with the sweet summer scents around us and the fumes of the sweet, golden wine seemed to lift us a finger's breadth above the turf and hold us suspended.
—EVELYN WAUGH

Good friends, good food, good wine, and good weather—
doth a good picnic make.   —ANONYMOUS

Seating themselves on the green sward, they eat while the corks fly and there is talk, laughter and merriment, and perfect freedom, for the universe is their drawing room and the sun their lamp. Besides, they have appetite, Nature's special gift, which lends to such a meal a vivacity unknown indoors, however beautiful the surroundings.

—BRILLAT-SAVARIN

When the cold came before the snow, we went skating on Williams Lake across the Arm. Remembering her own childhood, my mother put hot baked potatoes in the boots of our skates. After the rowboat ferry ride, one oar almost touching the edge of the ice line on the half-frozen Arm, and the walk up to the lake, the skates were warm to put on and the potatoes cool enough to eat.

—ROBERT MACNEIL

Even an old boot tastes good if it is cooked over charcoal.

—ITALIAN FOLK SAYING

A shady spot takes his fancy; soft grass welcomes him, and the murmur of the nearby spring invites him to deposit in its cool waters the flask of wine destined to refresh him. Then, with calm contentment, he takes out of his knapsack the cold chicken and golden-crusted rolls packed for him by loving hands, and places them beside the wedge of Gruyere or Roquefort which is to serve as his dessert.

—BRILLAT-SAVARIN

Eggs

Eggs of an hour, bread of a day, wine of a year, a friend of thirty years. —ITALIAN PROVERB

The egg is to cuisine what the article is to speech.

—ANONYMOUS

He placed the letter on the pile beside his plate; and, having decapitated an egg, peered sharply into its interior as if hoping to surprise guilty secrets. —P. G. WODEHOUSE

Probably one of the most private things in the world is an egg until it is broken. —M.F.K. FISHER

Omelettes are not made without breaking eggs.

—ROBESPIERRE

I had an excellent repast—the best repast possible—which consisted simply of boiled eggs and bread and butter. It was the quality of these simple ingredients that made the occasion memorable. The eggs were so good that I am ashamed to say how many of them I consumed. . . . It might seem that an egg which has succeeded in being fresh has done all that can be reasonably expected of it. —HENRY JAMES

Alas! my child, where is the Pen
That can do justice to the Hen?
Like Royalty, she goes her way,
Laying foundations every day,
Though not for public buildings, yet
For Custard, Cake, and Omelette.
No wonder, child, we prize the Hen,
Whose Egg is mightier than the Pen.
—OLIVER HERFORD

I never see an egg brought on my table but I feel penetrated
with the wonderful change it would have undergone but for
my gluttony; it might have been a gentle, useful hen, leading her chickens with a care and vigilance which speaks
shame to many women.   —ST. JOHN DE CRÈVECOEUR

As everybody knows, there is only one infallible recipe for
the perfect omelette: your own.   —ELIZABETH DAVID

Be content that those who can make omelettes properly can
do nothing else.   —HILAIRE BELLOC

It was obvious that the egg had come first. There was something dignified about a silent passive egg, whereas Aunt
Irene found it difficult to envisage an angel bearing a hen—
which despite its undoubted merits, was a foolish and
largely intractable bird.   —ALICE THOMAS ELLIS

A hen is only an egg's way of making another egg.
—SAMUEL BUTLER

Hickety, pickety, my red hen
She lays eggs for gentlemen;
But you cannot persuade her with a gun or lariat
To come across for the proletariat.
　　　　—DOROTHY PARKER,
　　　　　to G. K. Chesterton at dinner

Feasts and Celebrations

Hurrah for the fun! Is the turkey done?
Hurrah for the pumpkin pie!
—LYDIA MARIA CHILD

Our harvest being gotten in, our Governor sent four men on fowling, so that we might after a special manner rejoice together after we had gathered the fruit of our labor. They four in one day killed as much fowl as, with a little help beside, served the company almost a week. At which time, amongst other recreations, we exercised our arms, many of the Indians coming among us, and among the rest their greatest King Massasoit, with some ninety men, whom for three days we entertained and feasted, and they went out and killed five deer, which they brought to the plantation and bestowed on our governor, and upon the captain, and others.
—EDWARD WINSLOW, recalling Thanksgiving celebration in Plymouth, 1621

The king and high priest of all the festivals was the autumn
Thanksgiving. When the apples were all gathered and the
cider was all made, and the yellow pumpkins were rolled
in from many a hill in billows of gold, and the corn was
husked, and the labors of the season were done, and the
warm, late days of Indian Summer came in, dreamy, and
calm, and still, with just enough frost to crisp the ground
of a morning, but with warm traces of benignant, sunny
hours at noon, there came over the community a sort of
genial repose of spirit—a sense of something accomplished.
—HARRIET BEECHER STOWE

The chickens we raised were also propitious. They were as
free-range as any *poularde de Bresse* and twice as big as a
Perdue. These were chickens to put meat on your bones,
and if they were old enough to be tough, we cooked them
long enough to weaken their resistance. A Christmas
chicken had to be big enough to serve six people one piece
each, with wings, back, neck, and pope's nose available
upon request. Nothing went to waste, including the wishbone. As the youngest, I claimed the wishbone as my birth-
right and let it dry on my butter plate during dinner so that
it would be brittle enough for wishing on after dessert. I
chose Grandfather for my wishmate because I knew that at
the last moment he would slip his thumb down his side of
the bone to break it first so that my wish would come true.
My wishbone wish was the same as my bedtime prayer:
"Make me a good girl and let me be happy." I was too
young to know what an oxymoron was.   —BETTY FUSSELL

There never was such a goose. Bob said he didn't believe there ever was such a goose cooked. Its tenderness and flavor, size and cheapness were the themes of universal admiration. Eked out by apple-sauce and mashed potatoes, it was a sufficient dinner for the whole family; indeed, as Mrs. Cratchit said with great delight (surveying one small atom of a bone upon the dish) they hadn't ate it all at last! Yet every one had had enough, and the youngest Cratchits in particular were steeped in sage and onion to the eyebrows.
—CHARLES DICKENS

For my grandfather it was not Christmas unless he had his *pichon*. I have never seen anyone eat pigeon or squab the way my grandfather did. I would watch with fascination as he consumed the birds in a methodical way, with a sense of perfection a surgeon would envy. Each bone was picked completely clean, and they had an almost polished look when he was finished. He would arrange them on his plate, again with a perfection that seemed almost architectural. His pigeon made him so happy. A great grin would spread over his face when he was finished, and he would nod to all of us at the table with a look we'd not see again until next Christmas, and his next pigeon.   —FELIPE ROJAS-LOMBARDI

In my experience, clever food is not appreciated at Christmas. It makes the little ones cry and the old ones nervous.
—JANE GRIGSON

The true essentials of a feast are only fun and feed.
—OLIVER WENDELL HOLMES

Though we eat little flesh and drink no wine,
Yet let's be merry; we'll have tea and toast;
Custards for supper, and an endless host
Of syllabubs and jellies and mince-pies,
And other such lady-like luxuries.
—PERCY BYSSHE SHELLEY

Now is the time for drinking, now is the time to beat the
earth with unfettered foot.   —HORACE

Food and Love

Whenever I get married, I start buying *Gourmet* magazine.
—NORA EPHRON

Marriage, as I have often remarked, is not merely sharing
one's fettucine but sharing the burden of finding the fettucine restaurant in the first place.   —CALVIN TRILLIN

There is no sight on earth more appealing than the sight of
a woman making dinner for someone she loves.
—THOMAS WOLFE

What better way to win a heart than to spend a lazy summer
afternoon in some shady and secluded country spot, a
stream meandering by at the foot of the grassy slope, a few
fleecy clouds floating over head, and a bright red-and-white

checkered cloth spread out, upon which sits the champagne, the fat wedge of *pâté de campagne*, the strawberries and cream?
—JOHN THORNE

A man taking basil from a woman will love her always.
—SIR THOMAS MORE

Don't let love interfere with your appetite. It never does with mine.
—ANTHONY TROLLOPE

Love is grand, but love with lukshen [noodles] is even better.
—YIDDISH PROVERB

Love and eggs are best when they are fresh.
—RUSSIAN PROVERB

Making love without love is like trying to make a soufflé without egg whites.
—SIMONE BECK

Jewish cuisine differs from that of my fathers in both philosophy and content, but in its preoccupation with food as a gesture of love, the two have much in common. If the price we pay for that gesture be a little pain in the night, a little agony on the bathroom scales, a prowl down dark corridors groping for the Bisodol—well, who said love was all roses without a thorn?
—RUSSELL BAKER

Comfort me with apples: for I am sick of love.
—THE SONG OF SOLOMON 2:4

The way to a man's heart is through his stomach.
—FANNY FERN

Young couples would hold hands while they ate a delicious *raie au beurre noir* or a *vol-au-vent*. Between bites of food they would exchange passionate kisses. No one sitting near pretended to notice, but everybody looked pleased, and there was a glow of happiness about the place. Gaston beamed. He used to say that love enhanced digestion. Sometimes a girl who had exchanged kisses with a man one day would come with another man the next day and kiss him just as passionately. Infatuations were short-lived, but they were violent. It was a very romantic Prix-Fixe [restaurant]. —JOSEPH WECHSBERG

During the Maytime storms, when streams of water gushed past the blurred windows, threatening to flood their last refuge, the lovers would light the stove and bake potatoes. The potatoes steamed, and the charred skins blackened their fingers. There was laughter in the basement, and in the garden the trees would shed broken twigs and white clusters of flowers after the rain. —MIKHAIL BULGAKOV

After a perfect meal we are more susceptible to the ecstasy of love than at any other time. —DR. HANS BAZLI

Food and Memory

She sent for one of those short, plump little cakes called "petites madeleines," which look as though they had been molded in the fluted scallop of the pilgrim's shell. And soon, mechanically, weary after a dull day with the prospect of a depressing morrow, I raised to my lips a spoonful of the cake. . . . A shudder ran through my whole body and I stopped, intent upon the extraordinary changes that were taking place.   —MARCEL PROUST

In the light of what Proust wrote with so mild a stimulus, it is the world's loss that he did not have a heartier appetite. On a dozen Gardiner's Island oysters, a bowl of clam chowder, a peck of steamers, some bay scallops, three sautéed soft-shelled crabs, a few ears of fresh-picked corn, a thin swordfish steak of generous area, a pair of lobsters, and a Long Island duck, he might have written a masterpiece.
                                                        —A. J. LIEBLING

Bourbon does for me what the piece of cake did for Proust.
                                                        —WALKER PERCY

I remember his showing me how to eat a peach by building a little white mountain of sugar and then dripping the peach into it.   —MARY MCCARTHY

I like to imagine, in consummation and resolution of those jangling chords, something as enduring, in retrospect, as the long table that on summer birthdays and namedays used to be laid for the afternoon chocolate out of doors, in an alley of birches, limes and maples at its debouchment on the smooth-sanded space of the garden proper that separated the park and the house. I see the tablecloth and the faces of the seated people sharing in the animation of light and shade beneath a moving, a fabulous foliage, exagger-

ated, no doubt, by the same faculty of impassioned com-
memoration, of ceaseless return, that makes me always
approach that banquet table from the outside, from the
depth of the park—not from the house—as if the mind, in
order to go back thither, had to do so with the silent steps
of a prodigal, faint with excitement. Through tremulous
prism, I distinguish the features of relatives and familiars,
mute lips serenely moving in forgotten speech. I see the
steam of the chocolate and the plates of blueberry tarts. I
note the small helicopter of a revolving samara that gently
descends upon the tablecloth, and, lying across the table,
an adolescent girl's bare arm indolently extended as far as
it will go, with its turquoise-veined underside turned up
to the flaky sunlight, the palm open in lazy expectation of
something—perhaps the nutcracker.   —VLADIMIR NABOKOV

There was a particular kind of wheaten biscuit with a very
pale pure unsweetened flavor—I am reminded now of the
Host—which only my mother had the right to eat. They
were kept in a special biscuit tin in her bedroom and sometimes as a favor I was given one to eat dipped in milk. I
associated my mother with a remoteness, which I did not
resent, and with a smell of eau de cologne. If I could have
tasted her I am sure she would have tasted of wheaten
biscuits. . . . The wheaten biscuit remains for me a symbol
of her cool puritan beauty.   —GRAHAM GREENE

When from a long distant past nothing subsists, after the
people are dead, after the things are broken and scattered,
still, alone, more fragile, but with more vitality, more unsub-
stantial, more persistent, more faithful, the smell and taste

of things remain poised for a long time, like souls, ready to remind us, waiting and hoping for their moment, amid the ruins of all the rest; and bear unfaltering, in the almost palpable drop of their essence, the vast structure of recollection.

—MARCEL PROUST

I remember that at one time I saw two of my young mistresses and some lady visitors eating ginger cakes, in the yard. At that time those cakes seemed to me to be absolutely the most tempting and desirable things that I have ever seen; and I then and there resolved that, if I ever got free, the height of my ambition would be reached if I could get to the point where I could secure and eat ginger cakes in the way that I saw those ladies doing.

—BOOKER T. WASHINGTON

When I was seven or eight years old, my family took me to Birmingham to visit an aunt. I was born and raised in Mississippi during the Depression, and in that time and place anyone's idea of excitement or genuine adventure was a trip to a big town like Birmingham or Memphis. I remember— to tell the truth, it is the only thing I do remember about that trip—being taken to a Chinese restaurant. There were hanging Chinese lanterns and foreign waiters and real Chinese china and chopsticks and very hot and exotic tea. I cannot recall the menu in precise detail, but I did eat won ton soup and a dish that contained bean sprouts. I marveled over those bean sprouts. What an odd, enticing-looking vegetable! To this day I have not got over an inordinate fondness for won ton soup, and I have retained an all but insatiable appetite for any dish—even a mediocre dish—

made with bean sprouts. It is reasonable to suppose that the food I ate then was quite spurious, adapted to the Southern palate, and dreadful. But it kindled a flame.

—CRAIG CLAIBORNE

He was three years old when he took his earliest step in education; a lesson of color. The second followed soon; a lesson of taste. On December 3, 1841, he developed scarlet fever. For several days he was good as dead, reviving only under the careful nursing of his family. When he began to recover strength, about January 1, 1842, his hunger must have been stronger than any other pleasure or pain, for while in after life he retained not the faintest recollection of his illness, he remembered quite clearly his aunt entering the sick-room bearing in her hand a saucer with a baked apple.

—HENRY ADAMS

Then, as though touching her waist had reminded her of something, she felt in the pocket of her overalls and produced a small slab of chocolate. She broke it in half and gave one of the pieces to Winston. Even before he had taken it he knew by the smell that it was a very unusual chocolate. It was dark and shiny and wrapped in silver paper. Chocolate normally was dull-brown crumbly stuff that tasted, as nearly as one could describe it, like the smoke of a rubbish fire. But at some time or another he had tasted chocolate like the piece she had given him. The first whiff of its scent had stirred up some memory which he could not pin down, but which was powerful and troubling. —GEORGE ORWELL

Fruit

An apple is an excellent thing—until you have tried a peach!
—GEORGE DU MAURIER

Talking of Pleasure, this moment I was writing with one hand, and with the other holding to my Mouth a Nectarine—how good how fine. It went down all pulpy, slushy, oozy—all its delicious embonpoint melted down my throat like a large, beatified Strawberry.   —JOHN KEATS

There is greater relish for the earliest fruit of the season.
—MARTIAL

And every day when I've been good,
I get an orange after food.
—ROBERT LOUIS STEVENSON

The pear is the grandfather of the apple, its poor relation, a fallen aristocrat, the man-at-arms of our domains, which once, in our humid land, lived lonely and lordly, preserving the memory of its prestige by its haughty comportment.
—FRANÇOIS PIERRE
DE LA VARENNE

I love fruit, when it is expensive.

—SIR ARTHUR WING PINERO

My father cut down a magnificent plum tree which every year had given us a bountiful harvest of sweet juicy blue or red plums, I have forgotten which, and every second year or third year, I have forgotten which again, a bumper crop, in order to make room for a backyard garage. The car it contained was only a Maxwell. A whole fleet of Rolls Royces would not have compensated for the home-made fresh plum ice cream which disappeared with our tree.

—WAVERLEY ROOT

Garlic

It is not really an exaggeration to say that peace and happiness begin, geographically, where garlic is used in cooking.
—X. MARCEL BOULESTIN

There is no such thing as a little garlic.   —ARTHUR BAER

Garlic is the catsup of intellectuals.   —ANONYMOUS

>   Wel loved he garlek,
>   oynons, and eek lekes,
>   And for to drynken strong
>   wyn reed as blood.
>   —CHAUCER

Garlic Goes from Accessory to Star. Imagine a world without garlic. No spaghetti sauce. No veal parmigiana. No rata-

touille. No Chinese cooking, Italian cooking, or Greek cooking. No fun.   —SAVANNAH NEWS

There are many miracles in the world to be celebrated and,
for me, garlic is the most deserving.   —LEO BUSCAGLIA

All Italy is in the fine, penetrating smell; and all Provence;
and all Spain. An onion or garlic-scented atmosphere hovers
alike over the narrow calli of Venice, the cool courts of Cor-
dova, and the thronged amphitheatre of Arles. It is the only
atmosphere breathed by the Latin peoples of the South, so
that ever it must suggest blue skies and endless sunshine,
cypress groves and olive orchards. For the traveller it is
interwoven with memories of the golden canvases of Titian,
the song of Dante, the music of Mascagni.
                                        —ELIZABETH PENNELL

Garlick hath properties that make a man winke, drinke and
stinke.   —THOMAS NASHE

A nickel will get you on the subway, but garlic will get you
a seat.   —OLD NEW YORK YIDDISH SAYING

There's something about garlic that creates excitement. People can get real loose around garlic.   —LLOYD HARRIS

Garlic is as good as ten mothers.   —TELUGU PROVERB

And there was a cut of some roast . . . which was borne on
Pegasus-wings of garlic beyond mundane speculation.
                                             —C. S. FORESTER

Tomatoes and oregano make it Italian; wine and tarragon make it French. Sour cream makes it Russian; lemon and cinnamon make it Greek. Soy sauce makes it Chinese; garlic makes it good.   —ALICE MAY BROCK

Gluttony

O gluttony, it is to thee we owe our griefs!   —CHAUCER

A stomach that is seldom empty despises common food.
                                                    —HORACE

A fool that eats till he is sick must fast till he is well.
                                    —GEORGE WALTER THORNBURY

What suffering results from over-eating! Let man, then, drive from his heart and from his hand the idleness which finds its delights in blamable pleasures and cleave to moderation when he eats . . . for there are many among men who fail to hold the reins taut, but let them drop loosely upon their bellies.   —OPPIAN

Gluttony is an emotional escape, a sign something is eating us.   —PETER DE VRIES

Eat not to dullness. Drink not to elevation.
                                          —BENJAMIN FRANKLIN

He who distinguishes the true savor of his food can never
be a glutton; he who does not cannot be otherwise.

—HENRY DAVID THOREAU

[Almanzo] felt a little better when he sat down to the good
Sunday dinner. Mother sliced the hot rye'n'injun bread on
the bread-board by her plate. Father's spoon cut deep into
the chicken pie; he scooped out big pieces of thick crust and
turned up their fluffy yellow under-sides on the plate. He
poured gravy over them; he dipped up big pieces of tender
chicken, dark meat and white meat sliding from the bones.
He added a mound of baked beans and topped it with a
quivering slice of fat pork. At the edge of the plate he piled
dark-red beet pickles. And he handed the plate to Almanzo.

Silently Almanzo ate it all. Then he ate a piece of pumpkin pie, and he felt very full inside. But he ate a piece of apple pie with cheese. —LAURA INGALLS WILDER

89
Gour-
mets,
Gour-
mands,
and
Gastro-
nomes

Gourmets, Gourmands, and Gastronomes

A man who is rich in his adolescence is almost doomed to be a dilettante at table. This is not because all millionaires are stupid but because they are impelled to experiment. In learning to eat, as in psychoanalysis, the customer, in order to profit, must be sensible of the cost. —A. J. LIEBLING

I hate people who are not serious about their meals.
—OSCAR WILDE

To be a gourmet you must start early, as you must begin riding early to be a good horseman. You must live in France; your father must have been a gourmet. Nothing in life must interest you but your stomach. With hands trembling, you must approach the meal about which you have worried all day and risk dying of a stroke if it isn't perfect.
—LUDWIG BEMELMANS

A true gastronome should always be ready to eat, just as a soldier should always be ready to fight.
—CHARLES MONSELET

90

Gour-
mets,
Gour-
mands,
and
Gastro-
nomes

A gourmet is a being pleasing to heaven.

—CHARLES MONSELET

A gourmet who thinks of calories is like a tart who looks at her watch. —JAMES BEARD

Actually, the true gourmet, like the true artist, is one of the unhappiest creatures existent. His trouble comes from so seldom finding what he constantly seeks: perfection.

—LUDWIG BEMELMANS

Dr. Middleton misdoubted the future as well as the past of the man who did not, in becoming gravity, exult to dine. That man he deemed unfit for this world and the next.

—GEORGE MEREDITH

Hard Drink, Booze, and Liquor

Reminds me of my safari in Africa. Somebody forgot the corkscrew and for several days we had to live on nothing but food and water.
—W. C. FIELDS

It was my Uncle George who discovered that alcohol was a food well in advance of modern medical thought.
—P. G. WODEHOUSE

The standard of perfection for vodka (no color, no taste, no smell) was expounded to me long ago by the then Estonian consul-general in New York, and it accounts perfectly for the drink's rising popularity with those who like their alcohol in conjunction with the reassuring tastes of infancy—tomato juice, orange juice, chicken broth. It is the ideal intoxicant for the drinker who wants no reminder of how hurt Mother would be if she knew what he was doing.

—A. J. LIEBLING

Then imagine William Faulkner, having finished *Absalom, Absalom!*, drained, written out, pissed-off, feeling himself over the edge and out of it, nowhere, but he goes some-

where, his favorite hunting place in the delta wilderness of the Big Sunflower River and, still feeling bad with his hunting cronies and maybe even a little phony, which he was, what with him trying to pretend that he was one of them, a farmer, hunkered down in the cold and rain after the hunt, after honorably passing up does and seeing no bucks, shivering and snot-nosed, takes out a flat pint of any bourbon at all and flatfoots about a third of it. He shivers again but not from the cold.

—WALKER PERCY

Give me another drink and I'll tell you all you want to know.

—FATS WALLER

I hate to advocate drugs, alcohol, violence, or insanity to anyone, but they've always worked for me.

—HUNTER S. THOMPSON

Drink! for you know not whence you came, nor why; Drink! for you know not why you go, nor where.
—OMAR KHAYYAM

Drink because you are happy, but never because you are miserable.   —G. K. CHESTERTON

The young don't drink so much these days. In my day they were always throwing up in their top hats.
—ALICE-LEONE MOATS

I'm a Christian, but that doesn't mean I'm a long-faced square. I like a little Bourbon.   —LILLIAN CARTER

Everybody should believe in something; I believe I'll have another drink.   —VARIOUSLY ASCRIBED

There are two reasons for drinking: one is, when you are thirsty, to cure it; the other when you are not thirsty, to prevent it. . . . Prevention is better than cure.
—THOMAS LOVE PEACOCK

I drink when I have occasion, and sometimes when I have no occasion.   —CERVANTES

Even though a number of people have tried, no one has yet found a way to drink for a living.   —JEAN KERR

It was Mr. Western's custom every afternoon, as soon as he was drunk, to hear his daughter play upon the harpsichord.
—HENRY FIELDING

They all thought she was dead; but my father he kept ladling gin down her throat till she came to so sudden that she bit the bowl off the spoon.   —GEORGE BERNARD SHAW

> The man that isn't jolly after drinking
> Is just a drivelling idiot, to my thinking.
>   —EURIPEDES

There is absolutely no scientific proof of a trustworthy kind, that moderate consumption of sound alcoholic liquor does a healthy body any harm at all; while on the other hand there is the unbroken testimony of all history that alcoholic liquors have been used by the strongest, wisest, handsomest, and in every way best races of all times.

—GEORGE SAINTSBURY

On being warned that drink was "slow poison," Robert Benchley replied, "So who's in a hurry?"

—ROBERT BENCHLEY

Gin was mother's milk to her.   —GEORGE BERNARD SHAW

I never drink anything stronger than gin before breakfast.

—W. C. FIELDS

Often Daddy sat up very late working on a case of Scotch.

—ROBERT BENCHLEY

Anybody who hates dogs and loves whiskey can't be all bad.   —W. C. FIELDS

He that eateth well, drinketh well; he that drinketh well, sleepeth well; he that sleepeth well, sinneth not; he that sinneth not goeth straight through Purgatory to Paradise.
—WILLIAM LITHGOW

I'll eat when I'm hungry and drink when I'm dry,
If moonshine don't kill me, I'll live till I die.
—ANONYMOUS AMERICAN SONG

Claret is the liquor for boys; port for men; but he who aspires to be a hero must drink brandy.
—SAMUEL JOHNSON

Red wine for children, champagne for men, and brandy for soldiers.
—OTTO VON BISMARCK

Some men are like musical glasses,—to produce their finest tones you must keep them wet.
—SAMUEL TAYLOR COLERIDGE

What does drunkenness not accomplish? It unlocks secrets, confirms our hopes, urges the indolent into battle, lifts the burden from anxious minds, teaches new arts.   —HORACE

Licker talks mighty loud w'en it git loose fum de jug.
—JOEL CHANDLER HARRIS

I have taken more out of alcohol than alcohol has taken out of me.
—WINSTON CHURCHILL

Drinking when we are not thirsty and making love at all seasons, madam: that is all there is to distinguish us from other animals. —PIERRE DE BEAUMARCHAIS

Gin-and-water is the source of all my inspiration.
—LORD BYRON

There's no such thing as bad whiskey. Some whiskeys just happen to be better than others. But a man shouldn't fool with booze until he's fifty, and then he's a damn fool if he doesn't. —WILLIAM FAULKNER

A martini shaken, not stirred. —IAN FLEMING

Drinking is in reality an occupation which employs a considerable portion of the time of many people; and to conduct it in the most rational and agreeable manner is one of the great arts of living. —JAMES BOSWELL

Drink helps us to penetrate the veil; it gives us glimpses of the Magi of creation where they sit weaving their spells and sowing their seeds of incantation to the flowing mind.
—DON MARQUIS

Not drunk is he who from the floor
Can rise alone and still drink more;
But drunk is he who prostrate lies
Without the power to move or rise.
—THOMAS LOVE PEACOCK

Only Irish coffee provides in a single glass all four essential food groups: alcohol, caffeine, sugar, and fat.

—ALEX LEVINE

I don't drink; I don't like it—it makes me feel good.

—OSCAR LEVANT

Home Cooking

Our home-cured ham was like nothing I have seen or tasted since. The difference between commercially smoked hams and those cured in the little slant-roofed brick shanty out behind our house is traceable, I suspect, to the fact that the former are not smoked with corncobs. Some of the commercial houses burn hickory sticks, yes, but no corncobs. If you have ever smelled freshly shucked corncobs burning, you can imagine what that odor did to a ham.

—DELLA T. LUTES

She [my mother] could make jello, for instance, with sliced peaches hanging in it, peaches just suspended there, in defiance of the law of gravity. She could bake a cake that tasted like a banana. Weeping, suffering, she grated her own horseradish, rather than buy the pishachs they sold in a bottle at the delicatessen. She watched the butcher, as she put it, "like a hawk," to be certain that he did not forget to put her chopped meat through the kosher grinder.

—PHILIP ROTH

Grandmother's favorite utensil was her wooden pudding
stick. The pudding stick began like a regular spoon with a
long handle but in place of a bowl was a block of wood two
or three inches in size. Grandmother had forgotten where
she got her stick but she was sure that it was the perfect
implement for stirring hasty pudding, the corn meal mush
that was Sunday night supper from September to June.

As small children, my cousins and I liked to watch Grandmother make the pudding. Once the kitchen fire was roar-
ing, she removed a stove lid and set an iron pot filled with
two quarts of water over the flames. After the water was
boiling she stirred in the cereal mixture. She stirred the brew
constantly with the pudding stick until the pudding was

thick. The yellow pudding, poured into soup plates, covered with rich milk, and sweetened with maple syrup, was, as Grandfather used to say, a "supper fit for a king."

—ESTHER E. WOOD

I have always thought that there is no more fruitful source of family discontent than badly cooked dinners and untidy ways.

—MRS. ISABELLA BEETON

The potato and leek soup that is prepared night after night in the kitchens of nearly every Parisian *concièrge* and in the kitchens of nearly every Ilé de France working family is nothing more than potatoes and leeks more or less finely sliced or cut up, depending on the *bonne femme*, boiled in salted water, and served, a piece of butter being either added then to the soup or being put to join the inevitable crust of bread in the soup plate before the boiled vegetables are poured over. It carries within it always the message of well-being and, were my vice and my curiosity more restrained, I, too, would adore to eat it every evening of my life.

—RICHARD OLNEY

At this point in the meal, the stomach was ready for serious eating, and I prepared beans with bacon grease, a dish I perfected in 1937 while developing my *cuisine du depression*. The dish is started by placing a pan over a very high flame until it becomes dangerously hot. A can of Heinz's pork and beans is then emptied into the pan and allowed to char until it reaches the consistency of hardened concrete. Three strips of bacon are fried to crisps, and when the beans have formed huge dense clots firmly welded to the pan, the bacon grease is poured in and stirred vigorously with a large screwdriver. . . . The correct drink with this dish is a straight shot of room-temperature gin. I had a Gilbey's 1975, which was superb.   —RUSSELL BAKER

If pale beans bubble for you in a red earthenware pot
You can oft decline the dinners of sumptuous hosts.
                                        —MARTIAL

All millionaires love a baked apple.   —RONALD FIRBANK

It may not be a dish for every occasion, but when it comes to those American foods that somehow always evoke casual warmth, wholesome relaxation, and goodwill, a toothsome hash served with green salad, fresh bread, and premium beer is still pretty hard to beat.   —JAMES VILLAS

Things taste better in small houses.   —QUEEN VICTORIA

Talk of joy: there may be things better than beef stew and baked potatoes and home-made bread—there may be.
                                        —DAVID GRAYSON

Next to getting warm and keeping warm, dinner and supper were the most interesting things we had to think about. Our lives centered around warmth and food and the return of the men at nightfall.   —WILLA CATHER

I never see any home cooking. All I get is fancy stuff.
                                        —DUKE OF EDINBURGH

It is odd how all men develop the notion, as they grow older, that their mothers were wonderful cooks. I have yet to meet a man who will admit that his mother was a kitchen assassin and nearly poisoned him.   —ROBERTSON DAVIES

There is one thing more exasperating than a wife who can cook and won't and that's a wife who can't cook and will.
                                                        —ROBERT FROST

Then [Pa sat] down, as they urged him, and lifting the blanket cake on the untouched pile, he slipped from under it a section of the stack of hot, syrupy pancakes. . . . The pancakes were no ordinary buckwheat pancakes . . . the cakes were light as foam, soaked through with melted brown sugar.
                                                —LAURA INGALLS WILDER

Red beans and ricely yours,
            —Is the way LOUIS ARMSTRONG signed his letters

"Who inu hell," I said to myself, "want to try to make pies like Mother makes when it's so much simpler to let Mother make um inu first place?"   —HARRIETTE ARNOW

And the best bread was of my mother's own making—the best in all the land!   —SIR HENRY JAMES

Hospitality

A host is like a general: it takes a mishap to reveal his
genius. —HORACE

After the snacks came the dinner. Here the good-natured
host let himself go. As soon as he noticed that a guest had
only one piece of anything left, he immediately helped him
to another, saying as he did so "Neither men nor birds can
survive without pairing." If anyone had two morsels left,
he added a third, saying: "Two doesn't go far. God favors
the Trinity." If a guest had three morsels, the host would
say to him: "Where have you seen a cart on three wheels?
Or a house with three corners?" He had an apt phrase for
four morsels, and for five also. —NIKOLAI GOGOL

At table people enjoy one another; above all when one has
managed to enchant them. —FERNAND POINT

It is a very poor consolation to be told that the man who
has given one a bad dinner, or poor wine, is irreproachable
in private life. Even the cardinal virtues cannot atone for
half-cold entrées. —OSCAR WILDE

When a man is invited to dinner, he is disappointed if he
does not get something good. —SAMUEL JOHNSON

It's entirely too folksy to serve your own cookies in your own house at any time. —ALAN KOEHLER

Small cheer and great welcome makes a merry feast.
—SHAKESPEARE

The hostess must be like the duck—calm and unruffled on the surface, and paddling like hell underneath.
—ANONYMOUS

For a rich man the finest role in the world is that of host.
—GRIMOD DE LA REYNIÈRE

The pleasure in giving a dinner is mostly the pleasure of giving yourself. The effort you take is your way of showing your company that you care about them enough to give them a good time. —MARGUERITE KELLY AND ELIA PARSONS

Nobody can really taste food unless he's had a good look at it first. —ALAN KOEHLER

Who depends upon another's table often dines late.
—JOHN RAY

Be attentive and receptive to guests. A true man expresses his dignity not only in combat, but how he treats his fellow human. You can be dying from fatigue, but never let it show to a guest. Always be modest about yourself and curious about the guest. —KAZAKH SAYING

Hospitality consists in a little fire, a little food, and an immense quiet. —RALPH WALDO EMERSON

Give the guest food to eat even though you yourself are starving. —ARAB PROVERB

Modesty is unbecoming in a cook and only stimulates the critical faculties of guests. —ANNA HAYCROFT

Go along, go along quickly, and set all you have on the table for us. We don't want doughnuts, honey buns, poppy cakes, and other dainties; bring us a whole sheep, serve a goat and forty-year-old mead! And plenty of vodka, not vodka with all sorts of fancies, not with raisins and flavorings, but pure foaming vodka, that hisses and bubbles like mad. —NIKOLAI GOGOL

Hunger

An empty stomach is not a good political advisor. —ALBERT EINSTEIN

The village seemed little changed from Napoleon's time: houses with pretty Russian window frames, horse-drawn sleds bearing timber and an old man carrying buckets of water on a yoke. And that great silence, save for the wind, of the Russian countryside. . . . As I left, the Bactura family pressed on me bread, salt pork fat, a handful of salt. I could not help thinking that Napoleon's starving soldiers, passing here, would have killed for such a gift. —JOHN J. PUTMAN

A good meal ought to begin with hunger.
—FRENCH PROVERB

He who wants to eat cannot sleep.   —BRILLAT-SAVARIN

Oliver Twist has asked for more.   —CHARLES DICKENS

This ravening fellow has a wolf in his belly.
—BEAUMONT AND FLETCHER

The best sauce in the world is hunger.   —CERVANTES

Hunger maketh hard beans sweet.   —JOHN HEYWOOD

The best of all sauces is hunger engendered by exercise in the open air, and, equally, the best of digestives is pleasant company.   —ST. ANGE

Hunger finds no fault with the cook.   —C. H. SPURGEON

As God is my witness, as God is my witness . . . I'm never going to be hungry again. No, nor any of my folks. If I have to steal or kill—as God is my witness, I'm never going to be hungry again. —MARGARET MITCHELL (Scarlett O'Hara, in *Gone With the Wind*)

The trouble with eating Italian food is that five or six days later you're hungry again.   —GEORGE MILLER

My stomach serves me instead of a clock.

—JONATHAN SWIFT

You cannot feed the hungry on statistics.

—DAVID LLOYD GEORGE

No man can be wise on an empty stomach.

—GEORGE ELIOT

I Hate It

Hate of the millions who've choked you down.
In country kitchen or house in town,
We love a thousand, we hate but one,
With a hate more hot than the hate of the Gun
—Bread Pudding!

—BERT LESTON TAYLOR

At this moment I bit into one of my frankfurters, and—Christ! I can't honestly say that I'd expected the thing to have a pleasant taste. I'd expected it to taste of nothing, like the roll. But this—well, it was quite an experience. Let me try and describe it to you.

The frankfurter had a rubber skin, of course, and my temporary teeth weren't much of a fit. I had to do a kind of sawing movement before I could get my teeth through the skin. And then suddenly—pop! The thing burst in my mouth like a rotten pear. A sort of horrible soft stuff was oozing over my tongue. But the taste! For a moment I just couldn't believe it! Then I rolled my tongue around it again and had another try. It was fish! A sausage, a thing calling itself a frankfurter filled with fish! I got up and walked straight out without touching my coffee. God knows what that might have tasted of. —GEORGE ORWELL

The French fried potato has become an inescapable horror in almost every public eating place in the country. "French fries," say the menus, but they are not French fries any longer. They are a furry-textured substance with the taste of plastic wood. —RUSSELL BAKER

I hate tomato roses, parsley on plates where no one will ever eat it, and any food gotten up to look like something else.
—BARBARA KAFKA

I hated myself because I smelt of onions and meat, and I seriously considered suicide in the cistern which supplied the house. —LOUISE DE KOVEN BOWEN

Custard: A detestable substance produced by a malevolent conspiracy of the hen, the cow, and the cook.
—AMBROSE BIERCE

Nor do I say it is filthy to eat potatoes. I do not ridicule the using of them as sauce. What I laugh at is, the idea of the use of them being a saving; of their going further than bread; of the cultivating of them in lieu of wheat adding to the human sustenance of a country. . . . As food for cattle, sheep or hogs, this is the worst of all the green and root crops; but of this I have said enough before; and therefore, I now dismiss the Potato with the hope, that I shall never again have to write the word, or see the thing.

—WILLIAM COBBETT

I say it's spinach, and I say the hell with it. —E. B. WHITE

I hate with a bitter hatred the names of lentils haricots— those pretentious cheats of the appetite, those tabulated humbugs, those certified aridities calling themselves human food!

—GEORGE GISSING

The meal was pretentious—a kind of beetroot soup with greasy *croûtons*; pork underdone with loud vulgar cabbage, potato croquettes, tinned peas in tiny jam-tart cases, watery gooseberry sauce; trifle made with a resinous wine, so jammy that all my teeth lit up at once.

—ANTHONY BURGESS

Madam, I have been looking for a person who disliked gravy all my life: let us swear eternal friendship.

—SYDNEY SMITH

In Darkest America

Americans, more than any other culture on earth, are cook-book cooks; we learn to make our meals not from any oral tradition, but from a text. The just-wed cook brings to the new household no carefully copied collection of the family's cherished recipes, but a spanking new edition of *Fannie Farmer* or *The Joy of Cooking*.   —JOHN THORNE

Canning gives the American family—especially in cities and factory towns—a kitchen garden where all good things grow, and where it is always harvest time. There are more tomatoes in a ten-cent can than could be bought in city markets for that sum when tomatoes are at their cheapest, and this is true of most other tinned foods. A regular Arabian Nights garden, where raspberries, apricots, olives and pineapples, are always ripe, grow side by side with peas, pumpkins, spinach; a garden with baked beans, wines and spaghetti bushes, and sauerkraut beds, and great cauldrons of hot soup.   —JAMES H. COLLINS

It is the Americans who have managed to crown minced beef as hamburger, and to send it round the world so that even the fussy French have taken to *le boeuf haché, le hambourgaire*.   —JULIA CHILD

They ate frozen meat, frozen fried potatoes and frozen peas. Blindfolded, one could not have identified the peas, and the only flavor the potatoes had was the flavor of soap. It was the monotonous fare of the besieged . . . but . . . where was the enemy? —JOHN CHEEVER

The breakfast food idea made its appearance in a little third-story room on the corner of 28th Street and Third Avenue, New York City. . . . My cooking facilities were very limited, [making it] very difficult to prepare cereals. It often occurred to me that it should be possible to purchase cereals at groceries already cooked and ready to eat, and I considered different ways in which this might be done. —J. H. KELLOGG

The Russian tourist in America is instructed to ask for the following in restaurants: "Please give me curds, sower cream, fried chicks, pulled bread and one jellyfish."
—THE RUSSIAN-ENGLISH PHRASEBOOK

The Americans are the grossest feeders of any civilized nation known. As a nation, their food is heavy, coarse, and indigestible, while it is taken in the least artificial forms that cookery will allow. The predominance of grease in the American kitchen, coupled with the habits of hearty eating, and the constant expectoration, are the causes of the diseases of the stomach which are so common in America.
—JAMES FENIMORE COOPER

I would rather live in Russia on black bread and vodka than in the United States at the best hotels. America knows nothing of food, love or art. —ISADORA DUNCAN

In America, the cow is on trial. The charges include dietary wrongdoing, pollution and misuse of natural resources.
—MOLLY O'NEILL

Americans can eat garbage, provided you sprinkle it liberally with ketchup, mustard, chili sauce, tabasco sauce, cayenne pepper, or any other condiment which destroys the original flavor of the dish. —HENRY MILLER

You can travel fifty thousand miles in America without once tasting a piece of good bread. —HENRY MILLER

It's Good for You

You have to eat oatmeal or you'll dry up. Anybody knows that. —KAY THOMPSON

Toast was a big item in my mother's culinary pharmacopeia. At first it was served plain and dry, but that was soon followed by crisp, sweet cinnamon toast, then baby-bland toast that tasted soothingly of fresh air. Thick slices of French toast, crisp and golden outside but moist and eggy within,

would probably come next, always topped with a melting knob of sweet butter and a dusting of confectioner's sugar. I knew I was close to recovery when I got the toast I liked best—almost-burned rye bread toast covered with salt butter.
—MIMI SHERATON

Mrs. Beaver stood with her back to the fire, eating her morning yogurt. She held the carton close to her chin and gobbled with a spoon. . . . "Heavens, how nasty this stuff is. I wish you'd take to it, John. . . . I don't know how I should get through my day without it."
—EVELYN WAUGH

Inhabitants of underdeveloped nations and victims of natural disasters are the only people who have ever been happy to see soybeans.
—FRAN LEBOWITZ

If my young master must needs have flesh, let it be but once a day, and of one sort at a meal. Plain beef, mutton, veal & chicken, without other sauce than hunger, is best; and great care should be used, that he eat *bread* plentifully, both alone and with everything else; and whatever he eats that is solid, make him chew it well. . . . If he at any time calls for victuals between meals, use him

nothing but *dry bread*. If he be hungry more than wanton, *bread* alone will down; and if he be not hungry, 'tis not fit he should eat.   —JOHN LOCKE

Back then, nobody knew about cholesterol, and a lot of our food was loaded with it. I still like dishes made with cream and butter. I shouldn't have them, and I'm told it's unhealthy, but *tant pis*.   —SIMONE BECK

Three [meals] a day are recommended. Call me crazy, but if you don't eat you will eventually die.   —JOHN ADLER

Yoghurt is very good for the stomach, the lumbar regions, appendicitis and apotheosis.   —EUGENE IONESCO

Pounding fragrant things—particularly garlic, basil, parsley—is a tremendous antidote to depression. But it applies also to juniper berries, coriander seeds and the grilled fruits of the chilli pepper. Pounding these things produces an alteration in one's being—from sighing with fatigue to inhaling with pleasure. The cheering effects of herbs and alliums cannot be too often reiterated. Virgil's appetite was probably improved equally by pounding garlic as by eating it.
                                            —PATIENCE GRAY

An apple a day keeps the doctor away.   —ANONYMOUS

I come from a very large family, very large—my mother raised 17 children. Fifteen of her own and two more. One of the things she used to say is, "Follow the cows, and whatever the cows eat, you bring back." We knew that the animals knew what was good to eat, and that's what we'd bring back. And this is one of the things that we were happy for. The animals knowing instinctively and by nature what was good for them to eat, well, we knew that that would be good for us as well. —PAUL ENCISO

If any man has drunk a little too deeply from the cup of physical pleasure; if he has spent too much time at his desk that should have been spent asleep; if his fine spirits have become temporarily dulled; if he finds the air too damp, the minutes too slow, and the atmosphere too heavy to withstand; if he is obsessed by a fixed idea which bars him from any freedom of thought: if he is any of these poor creatures, we say, let him be given a good pint of amber-flavoured chocolate . . . and marvels will be performed.
—BRILLAT-SAVARIN

All I ask of food is that it doesn't harm me.
—MICHAEL PALIN

All alcoholic drinks, rightly used, are good for body and soul alike, but as a restorative of both there is nothing like brandy. —GEORGE SAINTSBURY

Pulkheria Ivanovna was most entertaining when she led her guests to the *zakuska* [appetizer] table. "Now this," she would say, removing the stopper from a flask, "is vodka infused with St. John's wort and sage. If the small of your back or your shoulder blade aches, it really hits the spot. This vodka over here is made with centaury. If you've got a ringing in your ears or shingles on your face, it's just the thing. And this one's distilled from peach pits—here, take a glass, what a wonderful smell! If you've bumped your head and a lump's sprung up on your forehead, then all you have to do is drink a glassful before dinner. The minute you take your hand away, the lump will disappear, as if it had never been there at all."   —NIKOLAI GOGOL

The Joys of Drinking Wine

Think, for a moment, of an almost paper-white glass of liquid, just shot with greeny-gold, just tart on your tongue, full of wild-flower scents and spring-water freshness. And think of a burnt-amber fluid, as smooth as syrup in the glass, as fat as butter to smell and sea-deep with strange flavours. Both are wine. Wine is grape-juice. Every drop of liquid filling so many bottles has been drawn out of the ground by the roots of the vine. All these different drinks have at one time been sap in a stick. It is the first of many strange and some . . . mysterious circumstances which go to make wine not only the most delicious, but the most fascinating drink in the world.   —HUGH JOHNSON

Wine is bottled poetry.   —ROBERT LOUIS STEVENSON

Happy those children who are not made to blow out their stomachs with great glasses of red-tinted water during their

118

The
Joys of
Drink-
ing
Wine

meals! Wise those parents who measure out to their progeny a tiny glass of pure wine—and I mean "pure" in the noble sense of the word—and teach them: "Away from the meal table, you have the pump, the faucet, the spring, and the filter at your disposal. Water is for quenching thirst. Wine, according to its quality and the soil where it was grown, is a necessary tonic, a luxury, and a fitting tribute to good food." . . . It is no small thing to conceive a contempt, so early in life, not only for those who drink no wine at all but also those who drink too much. —COLETTE

> O, for a draught of vintage! that hath been
> Cool'd a long age in the deep-delv'd earth,
> Tasting of Flora and the country-green,
> Dance, and Provençal song, and sunburnt mirth!
> Oh, for a beaker of the warm South,
> Full of the true, the blushful Hippocrene,
> With beaded bubbles winking at the brim,
> And purple-stained mouth;
> That I might drink and leave the world unseen,
> And with thee fade away into the forest dim.
> —JOHN KEATS

It was during those tranquil evenings with Sebastian that I first made a serious acquaintance with wine and sowed the seed of that rich harvest which was to be my stay in many barren years. We would sit, he and I, in the Painted Parlour with three bottles open on the table and three glasses before each of us; Sebastian had found a book on wine tasting, and we followed its instructions in detail. We warmed the glass slightly at a candle, filled a third of it, swirled the wine round, nursed it in our hands, held it to the light, breathed it, sipped it, filled our mouths with it and rolled it over the tongue, ringing it on the palate like a coin on a counter, tilted our heads back and let it trickle down the throat. Then we talked of it and nibbled Bath Oliver biscuits, and passed on to another wine; then back to the first, then on to another, until all three wines were in circulation and the order of glasses got confused, and we fell out over which was which, and we passed the glasses to and fro between us until there were six glasses, some of them with mixed wines in them which we had filled from the wrong bottle, till we were obliged to start again with three clean glasses each, and the bottles were empty and our praise of them wilder and more exotic. —EVELYN WAUGH

Wine has a drastic, an astringent taste. I cannot help wincing as I drink. Ascent of flowers, radiance and heat, are distilled here to a fiery, yellow liquid. Just behind my shoulder-blades some dry thing, wide-eyed, gently closes, gradually lulls itself to sleep. This is rapture. This is relief.
—VIRGINIA WOOLF

120

The
Joys of
Drink-
ing
Wine

Then smile and a glass and a toast and a cheer,
For all the good wine, and we've some of it here.
—OLIVER WENDELL HOLMES

Wine makes daily living easier, less hurried, with fewer tensions and more tolerance. —BENJAMIN FRANKLIN

Happy, happy Burgundy! —ERASMUS

How I like claret! . . . It fills one's mouth with a gushing freshness, then goes down to cool and feverless; then, you do not feel it quarrelling with one's liver. No; 'tis rather a peace-maker, and lies as quiet as it did in the grape. Then it is as fragrant as the Queen Bee, and the more ethereal part mounts into the brain, not assaulting the cerebral apartments, like a bully looking for his trull, and hurrying from door to door, bouncing against the wainscott, but rather walks like Aladdin about his enchanted palace, so gently that you do not feel his step. —JOHN KEATS

I never drink—wine. —COUNT DRACULA

I was very well brought up. As first proof of so categorical a statement, I shall simply say that I was no more than three years old when my father poured out my first full liqueur glass of an amber colored wine which was sent up to him from the Midi, where he was born: the muscat of Frontignan.
   The sun breaking from behind clouds, a shock of sensuous pleasure, an illumination of my newborn tastebuds! This initiation ceremony rendered me worthy of wine for all time.
—COLETTE

"In vino veritas," said the sage. . . . Before Noah, men having only water to drink, could not find the truth. Accordingly . . . they became abominably wicked, and they were justly exterminated by the water they loved to drink. This good man, Noah, having seen that all his contemporaries had perished by this unpleasant drink, took a dislike to it; and God, to relieve his dryness, created the vine and revealed to him the art of making *le vin.* By the aid of this liquid he unveiled more and more truth.

—BENJAMIN FRANKLIN

A glass of good wine is a gracious creature, and reconciles poor mortality to itself, and that is what few things can do.

—SIR WALTER SCOTT

Connoisseur: A specialist who knows everything about something and nothing about anything. . . . An old wine-bibber having been smashed in a railway collision, some wine was poured on his lips to revive him. "Pauillac, 1873," he murmured and died.

—AMBROSE BIERCE

An aged Burgundy runs with a beardless Port. I cherish the fancy that Port speaks sentences of wisdom, Burgundy sings the inspired Ode.

—GEORGE MEREDITH

The dipsomaniac and the abstainer are not only both mistaken, but they both make the same mistake. They both regard wine as a drug and not as a drink.

—G. K. CHESTERTON

122

The
Joys of
Drink-
ing
Wine

The vine bears three kinds of grapes: the first of pleasure, the second of intoxication, the third of disgust.

—ANACHARSIS

The best wine is the oldest, the best water the newest.

—WILLIAM BLAKE

Every man at the beginning doth set forth good wine; and when men have well drunk, then that which is worse: but thou hast kept the good wine until now.   —JOHN 2:10

Wine is the pleasantest subject in the world to discuss. All its associations are with occasions when people are at their best; with relaxation, contentment, leisurely meals and the free flow of ideas.   —HUGH JOHNSON

Rice is born in water and must die with wine.

—ITALIAN PROVERB

Wine is sunlight, held together by water.   —GALILEO

From wine what sudden friendship springs!   —JOHN GAY

Chardonnay is a red wine masquerading as a white, and Pinot Noir is a white wine masquerading as a red.

—ANDRÉ TCHELISTCHEFF

Wine is the most healthful and most hygienic of beverages.

—LOUIS PASTEUR

I like best the wine drunk at the cost of others.
—DIOGENES, THE CYNIC

One barrel of wine can work more miracles than a church full of saints.
—ITALIAN PROVERB

Wine gives a man nothing. It neither gives him knowledge nor wit; it only animates a man, and enables him to bring out what a dread of the company has repressed. This is one of the disadvantages of wine: it makes a man mistake words for thoughts.
—SAMUEL JOHNSON

> I am beauty and love;
> I am friendship, the comforter;
> I am that which forgives and forgets.
> The Spirit of Wine.
> —W. E. HENLEY

Take counsel in wine, but resolve afterwards in water.
—BENJAMIN FRANKLIN

For a gourmet wine is not a drink but a condiment, provided that your host has chosen correctly.
—EDOUARD DE POMIANE

The wines that one remembers best are not necessarily the finest that one has tasted, and the highest quality may fail to delight so much as some far more humble beverage drunk in more favourable circumstances.
—H. WARNER ALLEN

124

The
Joys of
Drink-
ing
Wine

Burgundy for kings, champagne for duchesses, and claret for gentlemen.   —ANONYMOUS

Wine is man's most successful effort to translate the perishable into the permanent.   —JOHN ARLOTT

Wine is a precarious aphrodisiac, and its fumes have blighted many a mating.   —NORMAN DOUGLAS

I've got a motor-car and a basket of strawberries and a bottle of Château Peyraguey—which isn't a wine you've ever tasted, so don't pretend. It's heaven with strawberries.
                                                —EVELYN WAUGH

"Have some wine," the March Hare said in an encouraging tone. Alice looked around the table, but there was nothing on it but tea. "I don't see any wine," she remarked. "There isn't any," said the March Hare.   —LEWIS CARROLL

It was fascinating. He told me the precise part of the vineyard that each of the wines had come from, and why certain slopes produced lighter or heavier wines. Each wine we tasted was accompanied by an imaginary menu, described with much lip smacking and raising of the eyes to gastronomic heaven. We mentally consumed *ecrevisses,* salmon cooked with sorrel, rosemary flavored chicken from Bresse, roasted baby lamb with a creamy garlic sauce, an *estouffade* of beef and olives, a *daube,* loin of pork spiked with slivers of truffle. The wines tasted progressively better and became progressively more expensive; I was being traded up by an expert, and there was nothing to be done except sit back and enjoy it.   —PETER MAYLE

After a hard day's work there's nothing like a slice of properly chilled *foie gras* with a glass of fine Bordeaux before dinner. Too often people serve *foie gras* at the end of a rich meal when the stomach is tired and the palate doesn't appreciate its fine aroma. And never serve a salad with it! Nothing but a full-bodied, flavory, round, velvety, vintage claret deserves to be its companion. A Château Margaux 1899 or a Leoville-LasCases 1920 will do wonders for a fine *foie gras*—and vice versa.

—M. CHARLES BARBIER, quoted by Joseph Wechsberg

Fine wine must be treated like a lovely woman in bed.
                    —FRENCH PROVERB

Monsieur K. put the tips of his fingers together and gave the ceiling a contemplative stare. "People treat wine as if it were a soulless liquid. But wine is a living organism. Its cells act like the cells of a human being. Wine lives even when it seems to be dead in the bottle. Believe me, I've stopped going out to restaurants. I just can't stand the sight of a *type* called *sommelier* who wears around his neck a chain that ought to be tied to his leg. He's a

126

The
Joys of
Drink-
ing
Wine

criminal, a murderer! He swings a fine old bottle as though it were a soft-ball. He's never heard of the sediments, a sign of maturity and age, which develop over years of careful storing and must not be disturbed. He doesn't know that the cork must be drawn slowly and steadily, without haste or jerking. He forgets to clean the inside lip of the bottle with a white cloth and to sniff at the cork. Perhaps he knows that wine bottles are stored horizontally, and Cognacs and Armagnacs are not, because they would burn the cork. But does he know what a wine cellar should be like—clean, dark, well aired, but without drafts, and in a place that has no street trepidations. Ah, it is all very, very sad.

—JOSEPH WECHSBURG

Feast on wine or fast on water,
And your honor shall stand sure
  If an angel out of heaven
  Brings you something else to drink,
Thank him for his kind attentions,
Go and pour it down the sink.

—G. K. CHESTERTON

"I rather like bad wine," said Mr. Mountchesney; "one gets so bored with good wine."   —BENJAMIN DISRAELI

This wine should be eaten, it is too good to be drunk.

—JONATHAN SWIFT

Junk Food

I devoured hot-dogs in Baltimore 'way back in 1886, and
they were then very far from newfangled. . . . They contained precisely the same rubber, indigestible pseudo-
sausages that millions of Americans now eat, and they
leaked the same flabby, puerile mustard. Their single point
of difference lay in the fact that their covers were honest
German *Wecke* made of wheat-flour baked to crispiness, and
not the soggy rolls prevailing today, of ground acorns, plas-
ter-of-Paris, flecks of bath-sponge, and atmospheric air all
compact.

—H. L. MENCKEN

You can find your way across this country using burger
joints the way a navigator uses stars. . . . We have munched
Bridge burgers in the shadow of the Brooklyn Bridge and
Cable burgers hard by the Golden Gate, Dixie burgers in the
sunny South and Yankee Doodle burgers in the North. . . .
We had a Capitol Burger—guess where. And so help us, in
the inner courtyard of the Pentagon, a Penta burger.

—CHARLES KURALT

There's a lot more future in hamburgers than in baseball.
Baseball isn't baseball anymore.   —RAY KROC

Believe it or not, Americans eat 75 *acres* of pizza a day.

—BOYD MATSON

My mother's kitchen never housed a potato chip or a slice of white bread. Once in a while, I had a hot dog at another child's birthday party. Usually, guilt would make me confess the transgression. "You ate that junk?" my mother would say. Then she would shake her head as if I were reporting a pregnancy, wondering where she went wrong.

One rebels against such a mother. I rebelled against mine. I smoked cigarettes and I had affairs with Christians. But I never ate a Baby Ruth or drank a Coca-Cola.

—BETTY ROLLIN

Just Follow the Recipe

The dangerous person in the kitchen is the one who goes rigidly by weights, measurements, thermometers and scales. I would say once more that all these scientific implements are not of much use, the only exception being for making pastry and jams, where exact weights are important.

—X. MARCEL BOULESTIN

Take twelve to seventeen cockscombs, soak them in warm milk until the skins can be easily removed, wash them in cold water until the red pales to a surprising white, sprinkle them with lemon juice (Margaret used pickling liquor), roll the cockscombs in beaten egg, fry them briefly on both sides, and serve them, on rounds of celery root previously sauteed in butter, to any male who, as I did then, has trouble getting and keeping it up and displaying a cocky virility even when he has good reason to hang his head.

—GÜNTER GRASS

Obtain a gross of small white boxes such as are used for a bride's cake. Cut the turkey into small squares, roast, stuff, kill, boil, bake, and allow to skewer. Now we are ready to begin. Fill each box with a quantity of soup stock and pile in a handy place. As the liquid elapses, the prepared turkey is added until the guests arrive. The boxes delicately tied with white ribbons are then placed in the handbags of the ladies, or in the men's sidepockets. —F. SCOTT FITZGERALD

First prepare the soup of your choice and pour it into a bowl. Then, take the bowl and quickly turn it upside down on the cookie tray. Lift the bowl ever so gently so that the soup retains the shape of the bowl. *Gently* is the key word here. Then, with the knife cut the soup down the middle into halves, then quarters, and *gently* reassemble the soup into a cube. Some of the soup will run off onto the cookie tray. Lift this soup up by the corners and fold slowly into a cylindrical soup staff. Place the packet in your purse or inside coat pocket, and pack off to work. —STEVE MARTIN

The royal cooks who served Richard II began their instructions for making hash as follows:

Take hares and hew them to gobbetts . . .
Take conies [rabbits] and smite them to pieces . . .
Take chickens and ram them together.

—*THE FORME OF CURY,* 14th-century cookbook

Gently stir and blow the fire,
Lay the mutton down to roast,
Dress it quickly, I desire,
In the dripping put a toast,
That I hunger may remove—
Mutton is the meat I love.
On the dresser see it lie;
Oh, the charming white and red;
Finer meat ne'er met the eye,
On the sweetest grass it fed:
Let the jack go swiftly round,
Let me have it nice and brown'd.
On the table spread the cloth,
Let the knives be sharp and clean,
Pickles get and salad both,
Let them each be fresh and green.
With small beer, good ale and wine,
Oh ye gods! how I shall dine.

—JONATHAN SWIFT

A recipe for fish baked in ashes:

No cheese, no nonsense! Just place it tenderly in fig leaves
and tie them on top with a string; then push it under hot
ashes, bethinking thee wisely of the time when it is done,
and burn it not up.   —ARCHESTRATUS

Always have lobster sauce with salmon,
And put mint sauce your roasted lamb on.
Roast pork sans apple sauce, past doubt,
Is *Hamlet* with the Prince left out.

Nice oyster sauce gives zest to cod—
A fish, when fresh, to feast a god!
It gives true epicures the vapours
To see boiled mutton minus capers.
—ANONYMOUS

There is always a best way of doing everything, if it be to boil an egg. —RALPH WALDO EMERSON

Kitchens

Give me the provisions and whole apparatus of a kitchen,
and I would starve.   —MICHEL DE MONTAIGNE

The kitchen, reasonably enough, was the scene of my first
gastronomic adventure. I was on all fours. I crawled into
the vegetable bin, settled on a giant onion and ate it, skin
and all. It must have marked me for life, for I have never
ceased to love the hearty flavor of raw onions.

—JAMES BEARD

You better come on in my kitchen
'Cause it's going to be raining outdoors.
—ROBERT JOHNSON

Such a shelter as you would be glad to reach in a tempestu-
ous night, containing all the essentials of a house, and noth-

ing for housekeeping; where you could see all the treasures
of a house at one view, and everything hangs upon its peg
that a man could use; at once kitchen, pantry, parlor, cham-
ber, storehorse, and garret; where you could see so necessary a thing as a barrel or a ladder, so convenient a thing
as a cupboard, and hear the pot boil, and pay your respects
to the fire that cooks your dinner and the oven that bakes
your bread, and the necessary furniture and utensils are the
chief ornaments; where the washing is not put out, nor the
fire, nor the mistress, and perhaps you are sometimes
requested to move from off the trap door, when the cook
would descend into the cellar, and so learn whether the
ground is solid or hollow beneath you without stamping.

—HENRY DAVID THOREAU

And what a stove it was! Broad-
bosomed, ample, vast like a huge
fertile black mammal whose breasts
would suckle numberless eager
sprawling bubbling pots and pans.
It shone richly. Gazing upon this
generous expanse you felt that
from its source could emerge nothing that was not savory, nourishing, satisfying.   —EDNA FERBER

The big black six-burner stove,
wedged between an auxiliary corner
sink and the refrigerator, which we painted black, is the
reason, we sometimes tell each other, that we bought the
house. There were many, many reasons, of course, but the

compelling appeal of this generously proportioned stove, fueled by outdoor tanks of propane, is clearly evident as it sits stolidly, comfortably, on the terra-cotta tile floor. It seems to have been invented to turn out feasts for a gathered family.

—EVAN JONES

Our kitchen today is a rich, intoxicating blend of past, present, and future; basically it belongs to the past, when it was conceived and constructed. It is a strange and implausible room, dodolike to the modern eye but dear to ours, and far from dead. In fact, it teems with life of all sorts—cookery, husbandry, horticulture, canning, planning. It is an arsenal, a greenhouse, a surgical-dressing station, a doghouse, a bathhouse, a lounge, a library, a bakery, a cold-storage plant, a factory, and a bar, all rolled up into one gorgeous ball, or ballup. In it you can find the shotgun and shell for shooting up the whole place if it ever should become obsolete; in it you can find the molasses cookie if you decide just to sit down and leave everything the way it is. From morning till night, sounds drift from the kitchen, most of them familiar and comforting, some of them surprising and worth investigating. On days when warmth is the most important need of the human heart, the kitchen is the place you can find it; it dries the wet sock, it cools the hot little brain.

—E. B. WHITE

When I'm old and gray, I want to have a house by the sea. And paint. With a lot of wonderful chums, good music and booze around. And a damn good kitchen to cook in.

—AVA GARDNER

I saw him even now going the way of all flesh, that is to say towards the kitchen. —JOHN WEBSTER

We owe much to the fruitful meditation of our sages, but a sane view of life is, after all, elaborated mainly in the kitchen. —JOSEPH CONRAD

Some sensible person once remarked that you spend the whole of your life either in bed or in your shoes. Having done the best you can by the shoes and the bed, devote all the time and resources at your disposal to the building up of a fine kitchen. It will be, as it should be, the most comforting and comfortable room in the house.

—ELIZABETH DAVID

Last Words

Wish I had time for just one more bowl of chili.
—KIT CARSON

Doctor, do you think it could have been the sausage?
—PAUL CLAUDEL

I think I could eat one of Bellamy's veal pies.
—WILLIAM PITT

I feel the end approaching. Quick, bring me my dessert, coffee, and liqueur.
—PIERETTE BRILLAT-SAVARIN (the great gourmet's aunt)

Leftovers

The most remarkable thing about my mother is that for thirty years she served the family nothing but leftovers. The original meal has never been found.   —CALVIN TRILLIN

Rational habits permit of discarding nothing left over, and the use to which leftovers (and their economic allies, the wild things of nature) are put is often at the heart of a cooking's character.   —RICHARD OLNEY

The art of using up leftovers is not to be considered as the summit of culinary achievement.—*LAROUSSE GASTRONOMIQUE*

Never eat tomorrow what you can manage to eat today. A meal saved is a meal turned bad. It gets all yucky and horrible and then you can't eat it and if you do it makes you sick, you know what I mean?   —KEN ROBBINS

Every morning one must start from scratch, with nothing on the stoves. That is cuisine.   —FERNAND POINT

Luxuries

If it were not a pleasure, it would be an imperative duty to eat caviare . . . It is said that when sturgeon are in season, no less than two-thirds of the female consists of roe. It is certainly odd to think of a fish weighing perhaps 1,000 pounds being two-thirds made up of eggs. . . . At such a rate of reproduction, the world would soon become the abode of sturgeons alone, were it not that the roe is exceedingly good.

—E. S. DALLAS

Caviar is to dining what a sable coat is to a girl in evening dress.

—LUDWIG BEMELMANS

The roe of the Russian mother sturgeon has probably been present at more important international affairs than have all the Russian dignitaries of history combined. This seemingly simple article of diet has taken its place in the world along with pearls, sables, old silver, and Cellini cups.

—JAMES BEARD

Under cover of the clinking of water goblets and silverware and bone china, I paved my plate with chicken slices. Then I covered the chicken slices with caviar thickly as if I were spreading peanut butter on a piece of bread. Then I picked up the chicken slices in my fingers one by one, rolled them so the caviar wouldn't ooze off and ate them.

—SYLVIA PLATH

My idea of heaven is eating *pâtés de foie gras* to the sound of trumpets.

—SYDNEY SMITH

Melons

When one has tasted watermelons, one knows what angels eat. It was not a Southern watermelon that Eve took; we know it because she repented.　　　　　　　—MARK TWAIN

After he had shown us his garden, Peter trundled a load of watermelons up the hill in his wheelbarrow.

Peter put the melons in a row on the oilcloth-covered table and stood over them, brandishing a butcher knife. Before the blade got fairly into them, they split of their own ripeness, with a delicious sound. He gave us knives, but no plates, and the top of the table was soon swimming with juice and seeds. I had never seen anyone eat so many melons as Peter ate. He assured us that they were good for one—better than medicine; in his country [Russia] people lived on them at this time of year.　　　—WILLA CATHER

He who fills his stomach with melons is like him who fills it with light—there is a blessing in it.   —ARAB PROVERB

> Friends are like melons. Shall I tell you why?
> To find one good you must a hundred try.
>   —CLAUDE MERMET

> O precious food! Delight of the mouth!
> Oh, much better than gold, masterpiece of Apollo!
> O flower of all the fruits! O ravishing melon!
>   —MARC ANTOINE DE SAINT-AMANT

When you come for a visit, we'll give you melons the likes of which you've never tasted! And you'll find no better honey in any other village. Why, when we bring you the honeycomb, the scent fills the room! You can't imagine it, our honey is as pure as the Tsarina's tears, or the clear crystal of her earring. And the pies, what pies my old lady will feed you! If

you only knew, they're sugar, pure sugar! and the butter brims on your lips when you bite into them! Wizards these old ladies are! Did you ever drink kvass made from pears and blackthorn berries? Or vodka infused with raisins and plums? Have you eaten frumenty with milk? My friends, what glorious flavors there are in the world! Once you start eating, you can hardly stop. . . . But what am I prattling on

about? You'll just have to come see us, come soon! We'll
feed you such treats you'll tell all the world.
—NIKOLAI GOGOL

In watermelon sugar the deeds were done and done again
as my life is done in watermelon sugar.
—RICHARD BRAUTIGAN

Murder in the Kitchen

The carp was dead, killed, assassinated, murdered in the
first, second and third degree. Limp, I fell into a chair, with
my hands still unwashed reached for a cigarette, lighted it,
and waited for the police to come and take me into custody.
—ALICE B. TOKLAS

In general, only mute things are eaten alive—plants and
invertebrates. If oysters shrieked as they were pried open,
or squealed when jabbed with a fork, I doubt whether they
would be eaten alive. But as it is, thoughtful people quite
callously look for the muscular twitch as they drop lemon
juice on a poor oyster, to be sure that it is alive before they
eat it.
—MARSTON BATES

"Have sense," she said sharply, "lobsters are always boiled
alive. They must be." She caught up the lobster and laid it
on its back. It trembled. "They feel nothing," she said . . .

She lifted the lobster clear of the table. It had about thirty seconds to live.

Well, thought Belacqua, it's a quick death, God help us all.

It is not.

—SAMUEL BECKETT

Six white pigeons to be smothered, to be plucked to be cleaned and all this to be accomplished before Gertrude Stein returned for she didn't like to see work being done.

—ALICE B. TOKLAS

When we first began reading Dashiell Hammett, Gertrude Stein remarked that it was his modern note to have disposed of his victims before the story commenced. And so it is in the kitchen. Murder and sudden death seem as natural there as they should be anywhere else. . . . Food is far too pleasant to combine with horror. All the same, facts, even distasteful facts, must be accepted, and we shall see how, before any story of cooking begins, crime is inevitable.

—ALICE B. TOKLAS

Mushrooms

In Russia, the use [of mushrooms] is universal, from the emperor to the beggar; and those who know what a delectable dish they make . . . need not be told that they are always welcome. . . . Many peasants live almost entirely upon

them, at some seasons of the year. In the summer afternoons, bands of village children may be seen searching for
them in the woods, with little baskets on their arms.

—ROBERT BRENNER

Life is too short to stuff a mushroom.   —SHIRLEY CONRAN

Nature alone is antique and the oldest art a mushroom.

—THOMAS CARLYLE

So in that part of France, and I'm sure in many others as
well, and in Poland, Italy, Czechoslovakia and so on, there
exists a large invisible community of mushroom-hunters.
The concentration of eyes downwards, the careful tread of
boots, require peace. Sunday is the occasion. Woods which
have been silent most of the week, come alive. The crackling
of dry twigs announces our presence to all the others whom
we cannot see, a more frequent shushing up of dead leaves,
then the triumphant shout of our daughter, who has found
the first girolles of the day. Maurice's dog squawks as we
all close in swiftly on the fruitful corner, with encouraging
noises for the sharp-eyed novice. Then we all spread out
again, and a busy silence returns. One is isolated, all sense
of time goes in the velvet warmth of the young trees. Suddenly some more girolles appear, or the moist brown head
of a cep, and without meaning to, I shout aloud.

—JANE GRIGSON

We were seduced at once by the little town [Senonches],
the hotel and the forest. We not only ordered lunch but
engaged rooms to spend the night. While waiting for lunch

to be cooked, we walked in the forest where Gertrude Stein, who had a good nose for mushrooms, found quantities of them. The cook would be able to tell us if they were edible. Once more a woman was presiding in the kitchen. She smiled when she saw what Gertrude Stein brought for her inspection and pointed to a large basket of them on the kitchen table, but said she would use those Gertrude Stein had found for what she was preparing for our lunch.

—ALICE B. TOKLAS

Tim, Jane, and I headed up the McKenzie River the next day into the forests of the Cascades to hunt Chanterelles. The sight of the golden-orange Chanterelle nestled in bright green moss beneath the giant Douglas Fir is about as glorious as anything could be. Chanterelles have veins on the underside instead of gills. The patterns traced by these veins are quite remarkable. A fresh Chanterelle is solid and meaty, with a pronounced aroma of apricots. The flesh is white and fibrous, looking exactly like cooked white meat of turkey. Raw, it tastes peppery, but when slowly simmered in butter and its own juices, perhaps with a touch of sherry and herbs, it achieves culinary distinction worthy of the finest table.

—ANDREW WEIL

Rainy weather would bring out these beautiful plants [mushrooms] in profusion under the firs, birches and aspens in our park, especially in its older part, east of the carriage road that divided the park in two. Its shady recesses would then harbor that special boletic reek which makes a Russian's nostrils dilate—a dark, dank, satisfying blend of damp moss, rich earth, rotting leaves. But one had to poke and

peer for a goodish while among the wet underwood before
something really nice, such as a family of bonneted baby
edulis or the marbled variety of scaber, could be discovered
and carefully teased out of the soil. —VLADIMIR NABOKOV

When picking mushrooms:
You never know unless you *know* you know. —JAY JACOBS

National Traits

We walked slowly along the rows of trestle tables, admiring the merciless French housewife at work. Unlike us, she is not content to look at the produce before buying. She gets to grips with it—squeezing aubergines, sniffing tomatoes, snapping the matchstick-thin haricots verts between her fingers, poking suspiciously into the damp green hearts of lettuces, tasting cheeses and olives—and, if they don't come up to her private standards, she will glare at the stall holder as if she has been betrayed before taking her custom elsewhere.   —Peter Mayle

Everything ends this way in France, everything. Weddings, christenings, duels, burials, swindlings, diplomatic affairs—everything is a pretext for a good dinner.   —Jean Anouilh

In Bordeaux, as in the rest of France, the marriage of food and wine is celebrating hundreds of years of happiness. If there is relatively little thrill or experimentation, well, that's the way it often is with successful long-term marriages. But there's plenty of the ease, comfort and pleasure of partners content with each other. —FLORENCE FABRICANT

Many Frenchmen, it seems, have a button labelled pot-au-feu. Press it, and you'll be swamped with nostalgia—cosy kitchen, fire on the hearth, pot bubbling as it hangs from the pot crane, mother flinging in vegetables, the pervading smell, the wonderful beef, wonderful mother, those were the days. —JANE GRIGSON

There is a certain expression that comes on a middle-to-upper income bracket Frenchman's face when he is about to *deguster* something really good, cheese, wine, any sort of culinary specialty, that starts out as a sudden interior break in the train of conversation. Silence; he is about to have a gastronomic experience. Then as the fork or glass nears his mouth, his eyes and ears seem to have blanked out; all is concentrated in the power of taste. There follows a stage when the critical faculties are gathering, the head is bent, eyes wander, lips and tongue are working over the evidence. At last comes the climactic moment of judgment, upon which may hang the mood of the meal and with it who knows what devious changes in the course of love, commerce or the body politic. The thing was poor or indifferent; the man shrugs, applies his napkin as though wiping out the whole experience, and goes on with what was interrupted, not quite relaxed; some sense of letdown, a slight disgruntlement lurks in the conversation. It was good, excellent, perfect, and oh what an expansion of frame and spirit; the chair will hardly hold him; he is not smiling, not just yet, but life is as he sits back gravely nodding, eager to look his companion and all the world in the eyes, and this time the napkin touches his lips like a chaste kiss, or a cleaning rag on an objet d'art. —ELEANOR CLARK

> But since he stood for England
> And knew what England means,
> Unless you give him bacon
> You must not give him beans.
> —G. K. CHESTERTON

We are to be on *The Messenger* three days; arriving at Cincinnati (barring accidents) on Monday morning. There are three meals a day. Breakfast at seven, dinner at half-past twelve, supper about six. At each, there are a great many small dishes and plates upon the table, with very little in them; so that although there is every appearance of a mighty "spread," there is seldom really more than a joint: except for those who fancy slices of beetroot, shreds of dried beef, complicated entanglements of yellow pickle; maize, Indian corn, apple-sauce and pumpkin. . . .

At dinner there is nothing to drink upon the table, but great jugs full of cold water. Nobody says anything at any meal, to anybody. All the passengers are very dismal, and seem to have tremendous secrets weighing on their minds. There is no conversation, no laughter, no cheerfulness, no sociality, except in spitting; and that is done in silent fellowship round the stove, when the meal is over. Every man sits down, dull and languid: swallows his fare as if break-

fasts, dinners and suppers, were necessities of nature never to be coupled with recreation or enjoyment; and having bolted his food in gloomy silence, bolts himself in the same state.
—CHARLES DICKENS

Corn flakes' connotations for us are of swiftness, sunshine, youth, and brightness. They are as crisp and snack-like as potato chips, sweetened and salted like junk food, yet hallowed by Milk, which always says "Mother." In North American culture nothing bathed in fresh milk can be threatening or bad. Corn flakes are light, and therefore can get away with being eaten cold, even for breakfast. They are modern and easy, yet already traditional; a fast-paced bachelor food which still manages to remain associated with childhood and with families. Eating them for breakfast is a habit known to many countries on earth yet universally recognized as typically American. Since the food which it eats provides a nation with its identity, corn flakes thus gains yet another claim to be considered an institution. There is no great distance between cultural "institutions" in this sense and the reverence and sacrality which characterized the attitude of the Indians to corn in pre-Columbian America.
—MARGARET VISSER

I used to think . . . that the English cook the way they do because, through sheer technical deficiency, they had not been able to master the art of cooking. I have discovered to

my stupefaction that the English cook that way because that
is the way they like it.   —WAVERLEY ROOT

"I think this calls for a drink," has long been one of our
national slogans.   —JAMES THURBER

> A Frenchman drinks his native wine,
> A German drinks his beer;
> An Englishman his 'alf-and-'alf
> Because it brings good cheer.
> The Scotsman drinks his whisky straight
> Because it brings on dizziness;
> An American has no choice at all—
> He drinks the whole damn business.
>   —ANONYMOUS

Necessities

First flowers on the table; then food.   —DANISH SAYING

Grub first, then ethics.   —BRECHT

Better is a dinner of herbs where love is than a fatted ox
and hatred with it.   —PROVERBS 15:17

Better is the life of a poor man in a cottage . . . than delicate
fare in another man's house; and better a dry morsel and

quietness therewith, than a house full of sacrifices with
strife.
                                                   —PROVERBS 17:1

Bread is like dresses, hats and shoes—in other words,
essential!
                                                   —EMILY POST

> Pray for peace and grace and spiritual food,
> For wisdom and guidance, for all these are good,
> But don't forget the potatoes.
>   —JOHN TYLER PETTEE

Nostalgia and Tradition

There are certain tastes which those who have never experienced them as children can neither understand nor cure:
who but an Englishman, for example, can know the delights
of stone-cold leathery toast for breakfast, or the wonders of
"Dead Man's Leg"?
                                                   —W. H. AUDEN

Oh the glorious town of Konotop glistened with fat! At the
market and at the station, behind long rows of tables were
mounds of lard of all kinds—smoked and unsmoked with a
good rind. There were rings of sausage: Cracow-style,
stuffed with large chunks of meat and pork fat, blood sausage, grain sausage with a smell so strong it inflamed a
man's glands. There was ham rimmed with fat, *kasha* cooked

thick with lamb suet and cut into rounds to resemble buns, and country sausage with gristle. The lard-sellers glistened in their greasy clothes, reflecting the rays of the sun.

I'd buy a ring of sausage for five kopecks and break it into pieces, eating it the way people at the market eat. I didn't even glance at the lamb, which cost only a kopeck and a half per pound, nor at the meat. Pork and fish were the best foods at the market, especially the dried searoach at two kopecks a piece, large chunks with fatty red backbone and roe. I liked to eat the pork and the fish with white bread. Or I'd buy a small suckling pig from the lard-seller for forty kopecks—already roasted, with a crisp brown rind stippled with fat. The rind, baked just right, crackled under my teeth. It was easy enough to consume the whole pig in secret from those at home, awaiting me for dinner.

In Konotop, among this Ukrainian fat and garlic, I grew.
—KAZIMAR MALEVICH

Our friend Amy, an American, [was] long a resident of Mexico but [was] determined to reconstruct in alien surroundings the traditional Christmas dinners of her youth. Describing the preparation of roast pig to her skilled Indian cook, she wound up with the announcement, "The pig is brought to table on plenty of greenery, with an apple in the mouth." The cook looked first baffled, then resentful, and finally burst out with a succession of "no's." Her employer persisted patiently with helpful gestures and increasing firmness. When the pig was served, she discovered that her cook could effect an entrée which surpassed her wildest expectations. There was plenty of greenery and a distinct

air of martyrdom; but the apple was clenched, not in the pig's mouth, but in that of the desperate cook!
—IRMA S. ROMBAUER AND MARION ROMBAUER BECKER

Nouvelle Cuisine

The *nouvelle cuisine* marked a turning-point. People suddenly understood that they could celebrate without ruining their health.
—ALAIN SENDERENS

Anyone who believes for one second that the nouvelle cuisine has had any impact on the way Americans eat in their homes is crazy. It has nothing to do with anyone except possibly ten people who have chefs and are silly enough to think raspberries go with meat and kiwi with shrimp.
—NORA EPHRON

. . . lobster pâté adrift in a sea of asparagus sauce (complete with a tomato rose), pheasant potpie with a dome of puff pastry and a mousse of watercress.
—JAMES BEARD

. . . flatfish mantled in a banana *coulis* laced with Amaretto and dusted with bitter chocolate . . .
—JAY JACOBS

. . . a few limpid slivers of moist and milky veal, spun round with a tracing of succulent sauce, accented with a few perfect ovals of baby carrot, a graceful arch of herb.

Each mouthful is so poignant, however, that our appetite, if not assuaged, is at least abashed. To be hungry before such food is as vulgar—as seemingly wrong—as feeling lust before the Venus de Milo. —JOHN THORNE

The first course arrived. Fallow had ordered a vegetable pâté. The pâté was a small pinkish semicircle with stalks of rhubarb arranged around it like rays. It was perched in the upper left-hand quadrant of a large plate. The plate seemed to be glazed with an odd Art Nouveau painting of a Spanish galleon on a reddish sea sailing toward the . . . sunset . . . but the setting sun was, in fact, the pâté, with its rhubarb rays, and the Spanish ship was not done in glaze at all but in different colors of sauce. It was a painting in sauce. Ruskin's plate contained a bed of flat green noodles carefully intertwined to create a basket weave, superimposed upon which was a flock of butterflies fashioned from pairs of mushroom slices, for the wings; pimientos, onion slices, shallots, and capers for the bodies, eyes, and antennae.

—TOM WOLFE

A plate doesn't have to be arranged like an abstract painting.
—LARRY FORGIONE

It's so beautifully arranged on the plate—you know some-one's fingers have been all over it. —JULIA CHILD

Nouvelle cuisine roughly translated means "I can't believe I spent $96 and I'm still hungry!" —MIKE KALINA

Old Food

Today, millions of Americans who sit munching popcorn before flickering movie screens, television sets, and fireplaces are following an ancient tradition. Throughout much of the hemisphere generations of Indians popped corn in earthen vessels and ate it around open fires. One-thousand-year-old specimens of the grain from ancient, musty Peruvian tombs still popped when heated!

—NICHOLAS P. HARDEMAN

About Fruit Cakes. Many people feel that these cakes improve greatly with age. When they are well saturated with alcoholic liquors, which raise the spirits and keep down the mold, and are buried in powdered sugar in tightly closed tins, they have been enjoyed as long as 25 years after baking.

—IRMA S. ROMBAUER AND MARION ROMBAUER BECKER

While an eon, as someone has observed, may be two people and a ham, a fruitcake is forever. —RUSSELL BAKER

The Olive

The whole Mediterranean, the sculpture, the palms, the gold breads, the bearded heroes, the wine, the ideas, the ships, the moonlight, the winged gorgons, the bronze men, the philosophers—all of it seems to rise in the sour, pungent smell of these black olives between the teeth. A taste older than meat, older than wine. A taste as old as cold water. —LAWRENCE DURRELL

It is quite affecting to observe how much the olive tree is to the country people. Its fruit supplies them with food, medicine and light; its leaves, winter fodder for the goats and sheep; it is their shelter from the heat and its branches and roots supply them with firewood. The olive tree is the peasant's all in all. —FREDERICA BREMER

The olive tree is surely the richest gift of Heaven. I can scarcely expect bread. —THOMAS JEFFERSON

Good oil, like good wine, is a gift from the gods. The grape and the olive are among the priceless benefactions of the soil, and were destined, each in its way, to promote the welfare of man. —GEORGE ELLWANGER

Nyons, itself, sheltered from the *mistral* wind by the low hills of Les Baronnies, is home to the most delicious olive in France. Small, oval and black, its dry yet buttery flavour has an intensity and almost wine-like taste unequalled anywhere. And, of course, the oil produced from these olives is superb. No matter that the oil has collected prizes and accolades for a century, your tongue and your palate will tell you that this is a classic among olive oils. It's not just a liquid that you slurp over salads or mix with lemon juice or wine vinegar; it is also a food with a flavour and consistency to be valued in its own right. One of my grandfathers swallowed a teaspoonful every day of his life.

—GERALDENE HOLT

The last dinner of each month, when money simply was not there to be stretched, called for a favorite of my grandmother: hot lemon tea served with a variety of olives called *throumbes* . . . and brown bread. —RENA SALAMAN

159

On
Fast-
ing,
Slim-
ming,
and Diet

On Fasting, Slimming, and Diet

Never eat more than you can lift.   —MISS PIGGY

It is wonderful, if we chose the right diet, what an extraordinarily small quantity would suffice.   —GANDHI

Fasting today makes the food good tomorrow.
          —GERMAN PROVERB

Fasting is a medicine.   —ST. JOHN CHRYSOSTOM

Young misses whut eats heavy mos' gener'ly doan never ketch husbands.
          —MARGARET MITCHELL (Mammy to Scarlett,
          in *Gone With the Wind*)

"How long does getting thin take?" Pooh asked anxiously.
          —A. A. MILNE

Let us eat and drink; for tomorrow we shall die.
          —ISAIAH 22:13

Eat, drink and be merry, for tomorrow we diet.
          —ANONYMOUS

160

On
Fast-
ing,
Slim-
ming,
and Diet

To lengthen thy life, lessen thy meals.

—BENJAMIN FRANKLIN

If you have formed the habit of checking on every new diet that comes along, you will find that, mercifully, they all blur together, leaving you with only one definite piece of information: french-fried potatoes are out. —JEAN KERR

> If you wish to grow thinner, diminish your dinner,
> And take to light claret instead of pale ale;
> Look down with an utter contempt upon butter
> And never touch bread till it's toasted—or stale.
> —H. S. LEIGH

On those who prescribe diets:

If they do no other good, they do this at least, that they prepare their patients betimes for death, by gradually undermining and cutting off their enjoyment of life.

—MICHEL DE MONTAIGNE

As an aside, I can tell you that if there's nothing wrong with you except fat it is easy to get thin. You eat and drink the same as always, only half. If you are handed a plate of food, leave half; if you have to help yourself, take half. After a while, if you are a perfectionist, you can consume half of that again. On the question of will-power, if that is a factor, you should think of will-power as something that never exists in the present tense, only in the future and the past. At one moment you have decided to do or refrain from

an action and the next moment you have already done or
refrained; it is the only way to deal with will-power.

—MURIEL SPARK

I never worry about diets. The only carrots that interest me
are the number you get in a diamond.   —MAE WEST

Life is too short for cuisine minceur and for diets. Dietetic
meals are like an opera without the orchestra.

—PAUL BOCUSE

Onions

There is in every cook's opinion
No savoury dish without an onion:
But lest your kissing should be spoiled
The onion must be thoroughly boiled.

—JONATHAN SWIFT

The onion is the truffle of the poor.   —ROBERT J. COURTINE

Potherbs in the autumn garden round the house
Of my friend the hermit behind his rough-cut
Timber gate. I never wrote and asked for them
But he's sent this basket full of Winter Onions, still
Damp with dew. Delicately grass-green bundles,

White jade small bulbs.
Chill threatens an old man's innards,
These will warm and comfort me.

—Tu Fu

An honest laborious Country-man,
with good Bread, Salt and a little
Parsley, will make a contented Meal
with a roasted Onion.

—John Evelyn

And most dear actors, eat no onion
nor garlic for we are to utter sweet
breath.   —Shakespeare

How beautiful and strong those buttered onions come to my nose!

—Charles Lamb

Let onion atoms lurk within the bowl
And (scarce suspected), animate the whole.

—Sydney Smith

"What are poireaux?"

"Leeks."

"It looks like long, green, quite big onions," young Tom
said. "Only it's not bright shiny like onions. It's dull shiny.
The leaves are green and the ends are white. You boil it
and eat it cold with olive oil and vinegar mixed with salt and
pepper. You eat the whole thing, top and all. It's delicious. I

believe I've eaten as much of it as maybe anyone in the world."
—ERNEST HEMINGWAY

Happy is said to be the family which can eat onions together. They are, for the time being, separate from the world, and have a harmony of aspiration.
—CHARLES DUDLEY WARNER

He liked to get a whole onion in the hollowed out heel of a loaf of French bread and eat it as if it were an apple. He had an extraordinary appetite for onions, the stronger the better, and said that "Good ale, raw onions, and no ladies" was the motto of his saloon.
—JOSEPH MITCHELL, describing John McSorley

The Pleasures of Eating

Now to the banquet we press;
  Now for the eggs, the ham,
Now for the mustard and cress,
  Now for the strawberry jam!
Now for the tea of our host,
  Now for the rollicking bun,
Now for the muffin and toast,
  Now for the gay Sally Lunn!
          —W. S. GILBERT

What should we be without our meals? They come to us in our joys and sorrows and are the most blessed break that dullness ever can know.   —ANONYMOUS

All's well that ends with a good meal.   —ARNOLD LOBEL

The art of dining well is no slight art, the pleasure not a slight pleasure. —MICHEL DE MONTAIGNE

Now hopping-john was F. Jasmine's very favorite food. She had always warned them to wave a plate of rice and peas before her nose when she was in her coffin, to make certain there was no mistake; for if a breath of life was left in her, she would sit up and eat, but if she smelled the hopping-john, and did not stir, then they could just nail down the coffin and be certain she was truly dead.
—CARSON McCULLERS

Who will join me in a dish of tripe? It soothes, appeases the anger of the outraged, stills the fear of death, and reminds us of tripe eaten in former days, when there was always a half-filled pot of it on the stove. —GÜNTER GRASS

The kulebyaka [coulibiac] must make your mouth water, it should be voluptuous, so to say, in all its glory. As you cut yourself a piece of it, you wink at it, and, your heart over-flowing with delight, you let your fingers pass over it. . . . Then you start eating it, and the butter drips like large tears, and the stuffing is succulent, luscious, there are eggs in it . . . and onions. . . . Yes, yes, you eat two pieces of kule-byaka at once . . . but the third piece you reserve for the soup.
—ANTON CHEKHOV

My family dumplings are sleek and seductive, yet stout and masculine. They taste of meat, yet of flour. They are wet, yet they are dry. They have weight, but they are light. Airy, yet substantial. Earth, air, fire, water; velvet and elastic! Meat, wheat and magic! They are our family glory!

—ROBERT P. TRISTRAM COFFIN

April: We are still on the threshold of Spring. The jolly lamb-kin, whose younger brothers leapt so artlessly onto our table in March, now gambols a hint more sedately, but his flesh is nearly as delicious. Grass will give him a new flavour, and nowhere in the world is better grass lamb to be found than in England. . . . May: Ducklings and Spring Chickens greet us in an ecstatic chorus, eager for their funereal couch of green peas.

—AMBROSE HEATH

Without bread, without wine, love is nothing.

—FRENCH PROVERB

I use the verb "to eat" here to denote a selective activity, as opposed to the passive acceptance and regular renewal of nourishment, learned in infancy. An automobile receiving fuel at a filling station or an infant at the breast cannot be said to eat, nor can a number of people at any time in their lives.

—A. J. LIEBLING

Even as the eye glistened and the mouth began to water at the sight of a noble roast of beef, all crisp and crackly in its cold brown succulence, the attention was diverted to a plump broiled chicken, whose brown and crackly tenderness fairly seemed to beg for the sweet and savory pillage of the tooth. But now a pungent and exciting fragrance would assail the nostrils: it was the smoked pink slices of an Aus-trian ham—should it be the brawny bully beef, now, or the juicy breast of a white tender pullet, or should it be the smoky pungency, the half nostalgic savor of the Austrian ham?   —THOMAS WOLFE

Strange to see how a good dinner and feasting reconciles everyone.   —SAMUEL PEPYS

There is no love sincerer than the love of food.
                                          —GEORGE BERNARD SHAW

"There's cold chicken inside it," replied the Rat briefly; "coldtonguecoldhamcoldbeefpickledgherkinssaladfrenchrolls cresssandwichespottedmeatgingerbeerlemonadesodawater—"
    "Oh stop, stop," cried the Mole in ecstasies: "This is too much!"   —KENNETH GRAHAME

A man is in general better pleased when he has a good dinner upon the table than when his wife talks Greek.
                                              —SAMUEL JOHNSON

    All human history attests
    That happiness for a man—the hungry sinner!
    Since Eve ate apples, much depends on dinner.
                                              —LORD BYRON

The discovery of a new dish does more for the happiness of mankind than the discovery of a star.
                                              —BRILLAT-SAVARIN

I look upon it, that he who does not mind his belly will hardly mind anything else. —SAMUEL JOHNSON

We may live without poetry, music and art;
We may live without conscience and live without heart;
We may live without friends; we may live without books;
But civilized man cannot live without cooks.
He may live without books—what is knowledge but grieving?
He may live without hope—what is hope but deceiving?
He may live without love,—what is passion but pining?
But where is the man that can live without dining?
—OWEN MEREDITH

A good meal in troubled times is always that much salvaged from disaster. —A. J. LIEBLING

If a man be sensible and one fine morning, while he is lying in bed, count at the tips of his fingers how many things in this life truly will give him enjoyment, invariably he will find food is the first one. —LIN YUTANG

A man's own dinner is to himself so important that he cannot bring himself to believe that it is a matter utterly indifferent to anyone else. —ANTHONY TROLLOPE

Every man should eat and drink, and enjoy the good of all his labour, it is the gift of God. —ECCLESIASTES 3:13

Laughter is brightest where food is best.   —IRISH PROVERB

If you are ever at a loss to support a flagging conversation, introduce the subject of eating.   —LEIGH HUNT

God could have created all food as a bland mixture of proper nutrients: something like wheat-germ, yoghurt and honey in a cake form, or some sort of fruit which would have contained everything necessary to good health. However pleasant the mild flavor might be, we cannot imagine eating just one single flavor all the time, the reason being that we have been created with taste buds, a delicate sense of smell, and a sensitive appreciation of and response to texture and colour.   —EDITH SCHAEFFER

I always try to make every meal *une petite merveille.*
                                              —FERNAND POINT

A meal is an artistic social construct, ordering the foodstuffs which comprise it into a complex dramatic whole, as a play organizes actions and words into component parts such as acts, scenes, speeches, dialogues, entrances, and exits, all in the sequences designed for them. However humble it may be, a meal has a definite plot, the intention of which is to intrigue, stimulate, and satisfy.   —MARGARET VISSER

In many ways, chopsticks are the culinary equivalent of the stick shift. They enhance the act of eating and make it more participatory, tactile, not to mention fun. They give a certain ceremony to consumption and force the calorie-conscious diner to focus on the ritual of gustation, and therefore on the amount of food being shoveled into the mouth at any time.

This increased awareness, in turn, enhances the attention paid to whatever is being eaten and encourages the diner to focus more on flavor.　　　　　—DENA KLEIMAN

The joys of the table are superior to all other pleasures, notably those of personal adornment, of drinking and of love, and those procured by perfumes and by music.
　　　　　—HASSAN EL BAGHADADI

Political Food

If you can't stand the heat, get out of the kitchen.
　　　　　—HARRY S. TRUMAN

Eating and sleeping are a waste of time.　　—GERALD FORD

If a man is what he eats, what is George Bush? Among the President's favorite between-meal snacks: pork rinds swimming in hot sauce; shredded wheat laced with crushed Butterfinger bars [candy bar]; pigs-in-a-blanket doused with Cheez Whiz; and frankfurters followed by boiled shrimp and nachos. Bush also likes to stoke his martinis with as many as four olives—and to gobble any olives his cocktail-hour guests don't eat.　　　　　—*TIME* MAGAZINE

My favorite sandwich is peanut butter, baloney, cheddar cheese, lettuce and mayonnaise on toasted bread with catsup on the side. —SENATOR HUBERT HUMPHREY

We had the first of a very relaxed and informal series of meals with our family. Earlier, when Rosalynn was visiting the White House, some of our staff asked the chef and cooks if they thought that they could prepare the kind of meals which we enjoyed in the South, and the cook said, "Yes, Ma'am, we've been fixing that kind of food for the servants for a long time!" —PRESIDENT JIMMY CARTER, diary entry

Richard Nixon . . . committed unspeakable acts with cottage cheese. —JAY JACOBS

The ancient Goths of Germany had a wise custom of debating everything of importance to their state twice; that is, once drunk and once sober. Drunk, that their councils might not want vigor; and sober, that they might not want discretion. —LAURENCE STERNE

Because of the media hype and woefully inadequate information, too many people nowadays are deathly afraid of their food, and what does fear of food do to the digestive system? I am sure that an unhappy or suspicious stomach, constricted and uneasy with worry, cannot digest properly. And if digestion is poor, the whole body politic suffers. —JULIA CHILD

Asked to state his position on whiskey, the Congressman replied: "If you mean the demon drink that poisons the

mind, pollutes the body, desecrates family life and inflames sinners, then I'm against it. But if you mean the elixir of Christmas cheer, the shield against winter chill, the taxable potion that puts needed funds into public coffers to comfort little crippled children, then I'm for it. This is my position, and I will not compromise."
—ANONYMOUS

Praising the Pig

Everything in a pig is good. What ingratitude has permitted his name to become a term of opprobrium?
—GRIMOD DE LA REYNIÈRE

But I will place this carefully fed pig
Within the crackling oven; and, I pray,
What nicer dish can e'er be given to a man?
—AESCHYLUS

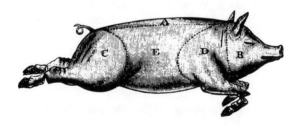

He must be roasted. . . . There is no flavor comparable, I will contend, to that of the crisp, tawny, well-watched, not over-roasted, *crackling,* as it is well called—the very teeth are invited to their share of the pleasure at this banquet in over-coming the coy, brittle resistance—with the adhesive oleagi-nous—O call it not fat! but an indefinable sweetness growing up to it—the tender blossoming of fat—fat cropped in the bud—taken in the shoot—in the first innocence—the cream and quintessence of the child-pig's yet pure food—the lean, no lean, but a kind of animal manna—or rather, fat and lean (if it must be so) so blended and running into each other, that both together make but one ambrosian result or common substance. —CHARLES LAMB

Pork is the real hero of the feast. Like a passionate youth it puts on different disguises on different occasions. But even clothed in the most elaborate attire its originality and genius is always revealed—whether we search it out under the drapes of a blood sausage, or in the sailor's jacket of liver-wurst, under the rough mantle of country sausage, or in the mantilla of a frankfurter. —NIKITA VSELOLZHSKY

What a world of gammon and spinach it is, though, ain't it? —CHARLES DICKENS

Nothing helps scenery like ham and eggs. —MARK TWAIN

I have never regretted Paradise Lost since I discovered that it contained no eggs-and-bacon. —DOROTHY SAYERS

Carve a ham as if you were shaving the face of a friend. —HENRI CHARPENTIER

Preserving the Bounty

All day . . . Auntie Dasha spent in making cherry preserves
in the garden . . . with a very serious face as though she
were performing a religious rite. . . . The garden smelt of
hot cherries. The sun had set, the charcoal stove had been
carried away, but the pleasant sweetish smell still lingered
in the air.   —ANTON CHEKHOV

Few sights do more to restore a cook's equanimity, and
induce self-complacency than a cupboard ranged with jars
and bottles, polished and labelled, in which the scents and
flavors, colors and textures of summer kitchen garden, fall
orchard and hedgerow are distilled, imprisoned and perfected. No treasure hoard was ever come by so innocently,
assembled so lovingly, or dismantled so enjoyably. Biting
into a fat red strawberry, or a crisp young cucumber is a

delight, but to meet them again in mid-winter, bobbing in sugary syrup, or piquant with herbs and vinegar, is a luxury.
—JOCASTA INNES

For Pulkheria Ivanovna, housekeeping meant continually locking and unlocking the pantry, salting, drying, and preserving an endless number of fruits and vegetables. Her house was like a chemical laboratory. A fire was constantly tended under the apple tree; and the kettle or copper vat—filled with jam, jelly, or confections made with honey, and sugar, and I can hardly remember what else—was almost never removed from its iron tripod. . . . Pulkheria Ivanovna always liked to prepare more than was needed, to have some on hand, and so much stuff was preserved, salted, and dried, that it would have buried the entire estate, had not the maidservants eaten a good half of it, sneaking into the pantry and stuffing themselves to such an extent that for the rest of the day they'd groan and complain about their stomachs.
—NIKOLAI GOGOL

I chose my wife as she did her wedding gown, not for a fine glossy surface, but such qualities as would wear well. She could read any English book without much spelling: but for pickling, preserving and cookery, none could excel her.
—OLIVER GOLDSMITH

Alexandra often said that if her mother were cast upon a desert island, she would thank God for her deliverance, make a garden, and find something to preserve. Preserving was almost a mania with Mrs. Bergson. Stout as she was, she roamed the scrubby banks of Norway Creek looking for fox grapes and goose plums, like a wild creature in search of prey. She made a yellow jam of the insipid ground-cherries that grew on the prairie, flavoring it with lemon peel; and she made a sticky dark conserve of garden tomatoes. She had experimented even with the rank buffalo-pea, and she could not see a fine bronze cluster of them without shaking her head and murmuring, "What a pity!" When there was nothing more to preserve, she began to pickle.

—WILLA CATHER

Quiche

Real men don't eat quiche. —BRUCE FEIRSTEIN

[Before the 1970s] real men not only didn't eat quiche, [they] didn't eat much of anything that hadn't been hacked from a bovine quadruped and served in its simplest form, along with fried, baked, or mashed potatoes. —JAY JACOBS

It was not until the sixties and seventies that the dish called "quiche," with all its corruptions, became a kitchen cliché, at home and in take-out shops. —EVAN JONES

Pesto is the quiche of the '80s. —NORA EPHRON

Restaurants

I never eat in a restaurant that's over a hundred feet off the ground and won't stand still. —CALVIN TRILLIN

Automat—The first restaurant to make it possible for the poor man to enjoy food served under glass. —FRED ALLEN

Never trust the food in a restaurant on top of the tallest building in town that spends a lot of time folding napkins. —ANDY ROONEY

I met a keen observer who gave me a tip: "If you run across a restaurant where you often see priests eating with priests, or sporting girls with sporting girls, you may be confident that it is good. Those are two classes of people who like to eat well and get their money's worth." —A. J. LIEBLING

Did I tell you about Oscar [Wilde] at the restaurant?

During the rehearsal he went to a place with my brother to have some lunch. He ordered a watercress sandwich; which in due course was brought to him: not a thin, diaphanous green thing such as he had meant but a very stout satisfying article of food. This he ate with assumed disgust (but evident relish) and when he paid the waiter, he said: "Tell the cook of this restaurant with the compliments

of Mr. Oscar Wilde that these are the worst sandwiches in the whole world and that, when I ask for a watercress sandwich, I do not mean a loaf with a field in the middle of it."

—MAX BEERBOHM

Never eat at a place called Mom's.　　—NELSON ALGREN

The larger the pepper mill, the lousier the food.

—MIKE KALINA

There are some things I hate in restaurants. I hate pretension, which is best embodied in snotty waiters who convey
the message that you're not good enough to be served by
them. Flocked wallpaper, brocade, and fake antiques are
also good signs of pretension. I hate overcooked vegetables.
I hate soups that have not had intimate relations with
chicken or beef bones. I hate overstuffed plates and excesses
of butter, oil, and cream. I hate microwaved frozen quiche
and whipped cream from a can and fruit pies with mass-
produced cornstarch fillings. I hate restaurants that buy their
food ready-made instead of cooking it. I hate frozen french
fries and canned white asparagus. I hate restaurants that
revolve on top of towers. I hate menus that sound as if they
were written by sophomoric ad-agency types. I hate paying
$1.25 for a tea bag sitting on a saucer beside a cup (or pot)
of lukewarm water. I hate the snobbery of tableside flambés.
I hate restaurants that spend more money on the decorator
than on the chef and the kitchen. I hate surf and turf.

—JOANNE KATES

When you find a waiter who is a waiter and not an actor,
musician or poet, you've found a jewel. —ANDRÉ SOLTNER

Epitaph for a waiter:
"God finally caught his eye." —GEORGE S. KAUFMAN

Venite omnes qui stomacho laboratis, et ego restaurato vos.
[Come all ye who labor with the stomach, and I will restore
you.] —M. BOULANGER, on a sign outside the first
restaurant, a soup kitchen, in Paris 1765

I can't count the number of delectable hours I've spent in bars, the perfect places for the meditation and contemplation indispensable to life. . . . The bar . . . is an exercise in solitude. Above all else, it must be quiet, dark, very comfortable—and, contrary to modern mores, no music of any kind, no matter how faint. In sum, there should be no more than a dozen tables, and a clientele that doesn't like to talk.
—LUIS BUÑUEL

There is no private house in which people can enjoy themselves so well as at a capital tavern. Let there be ever so much grandeur, ever so much elegance, ever so much desire that everybody should be easy, in the nature of things, it cannot be: there must always be some degree of care and anxiety. . . . There is nothing which has yet been contrived by man by which so much happiness is produced as by a good tavern or inn.   —SAMUEL JOHNSON

The other customers [in the restaurant] were all French, people from the neighboring villages dressed in their clean, somber Sunday clothes, and one or two more sophisticated couples looking fashionably out of place in their boutique colors. At a big table in the corner, three generations of a family piled their plates high and wished each other *bon appétit*. One of the children, showing remarkable promise for a six-year-old gourmet, said that he preferred this pâté to the one he ate at home, and asked his grandmother for a taste of her wine. The family dog watched patiently by his side, knowing as all dogs do that children drop more food than adults.   —PETER MAYLE

Anybody who doesn't think that the best hamburger place in the world is in his home town is a sissy.

—CALVIN TRILLIN

He who has not been at a tavern knows not what a paradise it is. O holy tavern! O miraculous tavern!—holy, because no carking cares are there, nor weariness, nor pain; and miraculous, because of the spits, which of themselves turn round and round!

—ARETINO

Don't go into a restaurant for something you can do better at home.

—NICOLAS FREELING

A restaurant is a fantasy—a kind of living fantasy in which diners are the most important members of the cast.

—WARNER LEROY

Salads

To make a good salad is to be a brilliant diplomatist—the problem is entirely the same in both cases. To know how much oil one must mix with one's vinegar.

—OSCAR WILDE

What is more refreshing than salads when your appetite seems to have deserted you, or even after a capacious dinner—the nice, fresh, green, and crisp salad, full of life and health, which seems to invigorate the palate and dispose the masticating powers to a much larger duration. The herbaceous plants which exist fit for food for men, are more numerous than may be imagined, and when we reflect how many of these, for want of knowledge, are allowed to rot and decompose in the fields and gardens, we ought, without loss of time, to make ourselves acquainted with their different nature and forms, and vary our food as the season changes. —ALEXIS SOYER

According to the Spanish proverb, four persons are wanted to make a good salad: a spendthrift for oil, a miser for vinegar, a counsellor for salt, and a madman to stir all up.
—ABRAHAM HAYWARD

Lettuce cooleth the heat of the stomacke, called the heartburning; and helpeth it when it is troubled with choler: it quenches thirst and causeth sleepe.

Lettuce maketh a pleasant sallad, being eaten raw with vinegar, oile, and a little salt: but if it be boiled it is sooner digested, and nourisheth more. —JOHN GERARD

Lettuce is like conversation: it must be fresh and crisp, and so sparkling that you scarcely notice the bitter in it.
—CHARLES DUDLEY WARNER

It is said that the effect of eating too much lettuce is "soporific." —BEATRIX POTTER

A number of rare or newly experienced foods have been claimed to be aphrodisiacs. At one time this quality was even ascribed to the tomato. Re-

flect on that when you are next preparing the family
salad.   —JANE GRIGSON

Iceberg lettuce is perhaps the most aptly named plant in the
world, and should be avoided as though you were the
Titanic with a second chance.   —ALAN KOEHLER

He that sups upon salad, goes not to bed fasting.
                                              —THOMAS FULLER

> Oh herbaceous treat!
> 'Twould tempt the dying anchorite to eat;
> Back to the world he'd turn his fleeting soul,
> And plunge his fingers in the salad bowl;
> Serenely full the epicure would say,
> "Fate cannot harm me,—I have dined today."
>   —SYDNEY SMITH

Salt

Salt is born of the purest of parents: the sun and the sea.
                                              —PYTHAGORAS

Salt is the only rock directly consumed by man. It corrodes
but preserves, desiccates but is wrested from the water. It
has fascinated man for thousands of years not only as a
substance he prized and was willing to labour to obtain, but

also as a generator of poetic and of mythic meaning. The contradictions it embodies only intensify its power and its links with experience of the sacred.   —MARGARET VISSER

Salt is white and pure—there is something holy in salt.
                                                        —NATHANIEL HAWTHORNE

The precious salt, that gold of cookery!
For when its particles the palate thrill'd
The source of seasonings, charm of cookery! came.
                                                        —HESIOD

Salt seasons all things.   —JOHN FLORIO

Salt is the policeman of taste: it keeps the various flavors of a dish in order and restrains the stronger from tyrannizing over the weaker.   —MALCOLM DE CHAZAL

Salt . . . nothing is perfect without it; the health of every individual depends on it, being an ingredient in our blood; it is as much required to be partaken of as food or drink . . . and the great Author of all has bountifully provided the whole human race, in every clime and country, with it.
                                                        —ALEXIS SOYER

Sandwiches

America is a confirmed sandwich nation. Everywhere you go you find sandwich stands, sandwich shops, and nine out of ten people seem to stick to the sandwich-and-glass-of-milk or cup-of-coffee luncheon. America has developed variety in fillings, breads, and shapes, from the four-decker combination to the pale slab of white bread with a paper thin slice of meat and much floury gravy poured over all to a vast array of really good sandwiches that distinguish our menus.
—JAMES BEARD

The greatest American sandwich . . . is the famous "BLT."
—PAUL LEVY

There was one picnic we always looked forward to. Father took great pride in "cutting good sandwiches"—the bread was thin, and if there was roast beef inside them it was thickly spread with drippings from the roasting pan, and there was lots of horseradish and pepper on the meat. Sometimes the sandwiches were of sliced lamb and chutney—I can still feel the crunch of the mustard seeds in that chutney—or a crusty roll filled with good fatty ham with a hard-boiled egg and tomato to eat on the side—that was awkward because you had to juggle them and the tomato juice always squirted out across your lap.
—DIANA KENNEDY

Smorrebrod are dainty open-faced sandwiches, erotic sculptures of pink baby shrimp, cod roe, smoked eel or rare roast beef. Each is garnished with fresh mayonnaise, with olives, shaved carrots, fat salty capers or pickled beets. Through ice clean windows you watch them on their blankets of thin pumpernickel like naked bathers, open for admiration. I cannot choose, I cannot speak the language and so I point: those three, and that one, the lobster meat crisscrossed with curls of red onion, and the halibut with peaks of tartar sauce and diced black radish.   —IRA WOOD

Always it was a club sandwich, the toast brown and crisp, the turkey moist with mayonnaise, the bacon sharp and smoky. The sandwich sat in the center of the plate, each of its triangular quarters secured by a toothpick. Next to it, on a single leaf of Boston lettuce, were two small gherkins. I ate those first, getting them out of the way before starting on the milk. And then, either in solitary glory or with the kids whose families let them eat upstairs every day, I looked out over the boats rocking at their moorings and lazily worked my way through each triangle. The waiter called me "sir," the tablecloth was white—and I was very fond of sandwiches.   —VLADIMIR ESTRAGON

After dinner we walked through the galleria, past the other restaurants and the shops with their steel shutters down, and stopped at the little place where they sold sandwiches; ham and lettuce sandwiches and anchovy sandwiches made of very tiny brown glazed rolls and only about as long as your finger. They were to eat in the night when we were hungry.   —ERNEST HEMINGWAY

189

The
Savour
of
Burnt
Offer-
ings

The Savour of Burnt Offerings

We plan, we toil, we suffer—in the hope of what? A camel-load of idol's eyes? The title deeds of Radio City? The empire of Asia? A trip to the moon? No, no, no, no. Simply to wake up just in time to smell coffee and bacon and eggs. And, again I cry, how rarely it happens! But when it does happen—then what a moment, what a morning, what a delight!

—J. B. PRIESTLEY

Adam ate some breakfast. No kipper, he reflected, is ever as good as it smells; how this too earthly contact with flesh and bone spoiled the first happy exhilaration; if only one could live, as Jehovah was said to have done, on the savour of burnt offerings. He lay back for a little in his bed thinking about the smells of food, of the greasy horror of fried fish and the deeply moving smell that came from it; of the intoxicating breath of bakeries and the dullness of buns . . . He planned dinners, of enchanting aromatic foods that should be carried under the nose, snuffed and then thrown to the dogs . . . endless dinners, in which one could alternate flavour with flavour from sunset to dawn without satiety; while one breathed great draughts of the bouquet of old brandy.

—EVELYN WAUGH

190

The
Savour
of
Burnt
Offer-
ings

Hallo! A great deal of steam! The pudding was out of the copper. A smell like an eating-house and a pastrycook's next door to each other, with a laundress's next door to that. That was the pudding . . . like a speckled cannon-ball, so hard and firm, blazing in half of a half-a-quartern of ignited brandy, and bedight with Christmas holly stuck into the top. —CHARLES DICKENS

The smell of coffee cooking was a reason for growing up, because children were never allowed to have it and nothing haunted the nostrils all the way out to the barn as did the aroma of boiling coffee.
—EDNA LEWIS

I've long said that if I were about to be executed and were given a choice of my last meal, it would be bacon and eggs. There are few sights that appeal to me more than the streaks of lean and fat in a good side bacon, or the lovely round of pinkish meat framed in delicate white fat that is Canadian bacon. Nothing is quite as intoxicating as the smell of bacon frying in the morning, save perhaps the smell of coffee brewing. —JAMES BEARD

Seafood

Fish is held out to be one of the greatest luxuries of the table and not only necessary, but even indispensable at all dinners where there is any pretence to excellence or fashion.
—MRS. ISABELLA BEETON

If eels only looked a little less like eels more people would want to eat them.
—CLEMENT FREUD

Old Tray licked all the oysters up,
Puss never stood at crimps,
But munched the cod, and little Kit
Quite feasted on the shrimps.
—THOMAS HOOD

Want some sea food, mama!
Shrimpers and rice, that's very nice!
—FATS WALLER

Beelzebub himself could never keep a Capri fisherman out of a sea-cave if there was half a franc's worth of crabs inside it.
—NORMAN DOUGLAS

All the ingenious men, and all the scientific men, and all the imaginative men in the world could never invent, if all their wits were boiled into one, anything so curious and so ridiculous as the lobster. —CHARLES KINGSLEY

To the Rhenish winehouse at the Steelyard, and there eat a couple of lobsters and some prawns, and pretty merry.
—SAMUEL PEPYS, diary entry, May 2, 1665

My temples throb, my pulses boil,
I'm sick of song, and ode, and ballad—
So, Thyrsis, take the midnight oil,
And pour it on a lobster salad.
—THOMAS HOOD

CALVIN: I don't understand this business about death. If we're just going to die, what's the point of living?
HOBBES: Well, there's seafood . . . —BILL WATTERSON

Happy as a clam, sez you—
It surely gives me jitters,
To think my happiness will end
On a blue plate full of fritters.
—ANONYMOUS

They each wheeled their barrow
Through the streets broad and narrow,
Crying "Cockles and mussels, alive, alive-o!"
—OLD IRISH SONG

Agassiz *does* recommend authors to eat fish, because the phosphorus in it makes brains. But I cannot help you to a decision about the amount you need to eat. Perhaps a couple of whales would be enough. —MARK TWAIN

"Turbot, Sir," said the waiter, placing before me two fish-bones, two eyeballs, and a bit of black mackintosh.
—THOMAS EARLE WELBY

Fishiest of all fishy places was the Try Pots, which well deserved its name; for the pots were always boiling chowders. Chowder for breakfast, and chowder for dinner, and chowder for supper, till you began to look for fish-bones coming through your clothes. The area before the house was paved with clam-shells. Mrs. Hussey wore a polished necklace of codfish vertebrae; and Hosea Hussey had his account books bound in superior old shark-skin. There was a fish flavor to the milk too, which I could not at all account for, till one morning happening to take a stroll along the beach among some fishermen's boats, I saw Hosea's brindled cow feeding on fish remnant's, and marching along the sand with each foot in a cod's decapitated head, looking very slip-shod I assure ye. —HERMAN MELVILLE

Signs and Portents

Our Indian kill'd a Deer, & the other men some Turkeys, but the Indian begg'd very hard that our Cook might not boil the Venison & Turkey together, because it wou'd certainly spoil his luck in Hunting, & we shou'd repent it with fasting and Prayer.
—WILLIAM BYRD

To dream of cake foretells advancement for the laborer and enhancement for the industrious. . . . Those in love will be especially gratified. Layer cake denotes satisfaction. . . . A fluffy rich icing on a cake predicts gaiety.
—BALLANTYNE AND COELI

To see cucumbers in a dream denotes that you will speedily fall in love. Or, if you are in love, then you will marry the object of your affection. To dream that you are eating garlic denotes that you will discover hidden secrets and meet with some domestic jar. To dream that there is garlic in the house is lucky. To dream of lettuces is said to portend trouble . . . to dream of mushrooms denotes fleeting happiness, to dream you are gathering them, fickleness in a lover or consort. To dream of olives portends concord, liberty and dignity . . . parsley portends that you will be crossed in love . . . if you are eating it you will shortly hear good news. To dream of pumpkins is a very bad omen.
—RICHARD FOLKARD

Peace of mind and a comfortable income are predicted by a dream of eating potatoes in any form.
—BALLANTYNE AND COELI

According to superstition, empty egg-shells should always be broken up—lest witches make boats thereof.
—DOROTHY HARTLEY

Eating stew in a dream portends a reunion with old friends.
—BALLANTYNE AND COELI

Soup

Soup and fish explain half the emotions of life.
—SYDNEY SMITH

Beautiful soup, so rich and green
Waiting in a hot tureen!
Who for such dainties would not stoop?
Soup of the evening, beautiful soup!
Beautiful soup! Who cares for fish,
Game, or any other dish?
Who would not give all else for two
Pennyworth only of beautiful Soup!
—LEWIS CARROLL

Cold soup is a very tricky thing and it is the rare hostess who can carry it off. More often than not the dinner guest is left with the impression that had he only come a little earlier he could have gotten it while it was still hot.

—FRAN LEBOWITZ

Do you have a kinder, more adaptable friend in the food world than soup? Who soothes you when you are ill? Who refuses to leave you when you are impoverished and stretches its resources to give you a hearty sustenance and cheer? Who warms you in the winter and cools you in the summer? Yet who also is capable of doing honor to your richest table and impressing your most demanding guests? . . . Soup does its loyal best, no matter what undignified conditions are imposed upon it. You don't catch steak hanging around when you're poor and sick, do you?

—JUDITH MARTIN (MISS MANNERS)

Of soup and love, the first is best.   —SPANISH PROVERB

Of all the items on the menu, soup is that which exacts the most delicate perfection and the strictest attention.

—ESCOFFIER

But when that smoking chowder came in, the mystery was delightfully explained. Oh! sweet friends, hearken to me. It was made of small juicy clams, scarcely bigger than hazelnuts, mixed with pounded ship's biscuits and salted pork cut up into little flakes! the whole enriched with butter, and plentifully seasoned with pepper and salt . . . we despatched it with great expedition.   —HERMAN MELVILLE

This is not that, and that is certainly not this, and at the same time an oyster stew is not stewed, and although they are made of the same things and even cooked almost the same way, an oyster soup should never be called a stew, nor stew soup. —M.F.K. FISHER

I believe I once considerably scandalized her by declaring that clear soup was a more important factor in life than a clear conscience. —SAKI

Soup is cuisine's kindest course. —ANONYMOUS

It breathes reassurance, it offers consolation; after a weary day it promotes sociability. . . . There is nothing like a bowl of hot soup, its wisp of aromatic steam teasing the nostrils into quivering anticipation. —LOUIS P. DE GOUY

Only the pure of heart can make a good soup. —LUDWIG VAN BEETHOVEN

The best kind of onion soup is the simplest kind. —AMBROSE BIERCE

But even better is a borscht, prepared with beets, Ukrainian style, you know the way, my friend, with ham and country sausages. It should be served with sour cream, of course, and a sprinkling of fresh parsley and dill. —ANTON CHEKHOV

To make a good soup, the pot must only simmer, or "smile." —FRENCH PROVERB

In taking soup, it is necessary to avoid lifting too much in the spoon, or filling the mouth so full as almost to stop the breath. —ST. JOHN BAPTIST DE LA SALLE

Bouillabaisse is only good because cooked by the French, who, if they cared to try, could produce an excellent and nutritious substitute out of cigar stumps and empty match boxes. —NORMAN DOUGLAS

When she knew that he [Denys] was coming she would have his favorite dish for him. This was "clear soup," Kamante's exquisite consommé. Perhaps the making of this soup taught Karen Blixen something about writing stories. The recipe calls for you to keep the spirit but discard the substance of your rough ingredients: eggshells and raw bones, root vegetables and red meat. You then submit them, like a storyteller, to the "fire and patience." And the clarity comes at the end, a magic trick. —JUDITH THURMAN

Chowder breathes reassurance. It steams consolation. —CLEMENTINE PADDLEFORD

The great dish of New Orleans, and which it claims the honour of having invented, is the Gumbo. There is no dish which at the same time so tickles the palate, satisfies the appetite, furnishes the body with nutriment sufficient to

carry on the physical requirements, and costs so little, as a Creole gumbo. It is a dinner in itself, being soup, pièce de résistance and vegetable in one. Healthy, not heating to the stomach, and easy of digestion, it should grace every table.
—WILLIAM COLEMAN

> This Bouillabaisse a noble dish is—
> A sort of soup, or broth, or brew,
> Or hotchpotch of all sorts of fishes,
> That Greenwich never could outdo;
> Green herbs, red peppers, mussels, saffron,
> Soles, onions, garlic, roach and dace.
> —WILLIAM M. THACKERAY

Bouillabaisse, this golden soup, this incomparable golden soup which embodies and concentrates all the aromas of our shores and which permeates, like an ecstasy, the stomachs of astonished gastronomes. Bouillabaisse is one of those classic dishes whose glory has encircled the world, and the miracle consists of this: there are as many bouillabaisses as there are good chefs or *cordons bleus*. Each brings to his own version his special touch.
—CURNONSKY

The Sweet Things in Life

The only emperor is the emperor of ice-cream.
—WALLACE STEVENS

Once in a young lifetime one should be allowed to have as much sweetness as one can possibly want and hold.
—JUDITH OLNEY

I would stand transfixed before the windows of the confectioners' shops, fascinated by the luminous sparkle of candied fruits, the cloudy lustre of jellies, the kaleidoscope inflorescence of acidulated fruitdrops—red, green, orange, violet: I coveted the colours themselves as much as the pleasure they promised me. Mama used to grind sugared almonds for me in a mortar and mix the crunched powder with a yellow cream; the pink of the sweets used to shade off into exquisite nuances of colour, and I would dip an eager spoon into their brilliant sunset.
—SIMONE DE BEAUVOIR

The friendly cow, all red and white,
I love with all my heart;
She gives me cream with all her might,
To eat with apple-tart.
—ROBERT LOUIS STEVENSON

Wouldst thou both eat thy cake and have it?
—GEORGE HERBERT

And when dessert time came he himself brought to the table a wedding cake that drew exclamations from all. Its base was a square of blue cardboard representing a temple with porticoes and colonnades and adorned on all sides with stucco statuettes standing in niches spangled with gold paper stars. The second tier was a mediaeval castle in *gâteau de Savoie*, surrounded by miniature fortifications of angelica, almonds, raisins and orange sections. And finally, on the topmost layer—which was a green meadow, with rocks, jelly lakes, and boats of hazelnut shells—a little cupid was swinging in a chocolate swing. The tips of the two uprights, the highest points of the whole, were two real rosebuds.
—GUSTAVE FLAUBERT

Leave the gun. Take the cannolis.
—CLEMENZA, in the movie *The Godfather*

Dessert should close the meal gently and not in a pyrotechnic blaze of glory. No cultivated feeder, already well fed, thanks his host for confronting him with a dessert so elaborate that not to eat it is simply rude—like refusing to watch one's host blow up Bloomingdale's.   —ALAN KOEHLER

Mammy's cakes are so heavy the post office won't take them.   —ERNEST MATTHEW MICKLER

The rule is jam tomorrow and jam yesterday, but never jam today.   —LEWIS CARROLL

Coleridge holds that a man cannot have a pure mind who refuse apple-dumplings. I am not certain but what he is right.   —CHARLES LAMB

Fancy cream puffs so soon after breakfast. The very idea made one shudder. All the same, two minutes later José and Laura were licking their fingers with that absorbed inward look that comes only from whipped cream.
                                        —KATHERINE MANSFIELD

Oh, blackberry tart, with berries as big as your thumb, purple and black, and thick with juice, and a crust to endear them that will go to cream in your mouth, and both passing down with such a taste that will make you close your eyes and wish you might live forever in the wideness of that rich moment.   —RICHARD LLEWELLYN

Had I but a penny in the world, thou shouldst have it for gingerbread.   —SHAKESPEARE

If the people have no bread let them eat cake.
                                —Often ascribed to MARIE ANTOINETTE

Blessed be he that invented pudding, for it is a Manna that hits the Palates of all Sorts of People; a Manna better than that of the Wilderness, because the people are never weary of it.   —FRANÇOISE MAXIMILIEN

Few pleasures are greater than turning out a perfect cake. . . . Such creations can bring happiness to both our childhood and mature years, for few, if any, people are immune to their charm, and memories of them . . . lighten the dark corners of life.
—JOSEPH AMENDOLA AND DONALD E. LUNDBERG

The black stove, stoked with coal and firewood, glows like a lighted pumpkin. Eggbeaters whirl, spoons spin round in bowls of butter and sugar, vanilla sweetens the air, ginger spices it; melting, nose-tingling odors saturate the kitchen, suffuse the house, drift out to the world on puffs of chimney smoke. In four days our work is done. Thirty-one cakes, dampened with whiskey, bask on window sills and shelves.
—TRUMAN CAPOTE

I doubt whether the world holds for any one a more soul-stirring surprise than the first adventure with ice-cream.
—HEYWOOD BROUN

There is something in the red of a raspberry pie that looks as good to a man as the red in a sheep looks to a wolf.
—E. W. HOWE

A lot of people have never really had the chance to eat a decent apple pie, but after a minute's sensual reflection will know positively what they would expect if they did. They can taste it on their mind's tongue: thin flaky pastry and hunks of sweet apple bathed in syrup; rich but sturdy dough filled with finely sliced tart apples seasoned with cinnamon; an upper and lower crust in a traditional pie pan; an upper crust only, in a deep dish; a bottom crust with crosses of dough over the filling. —M.F.K. FISHER

Good apple pies are a considerable part of our domestic happiness. —JANE AUSTEN, in a letter

A house is beautiful not because of its walls, but because of its cakes. —OLD RUSSIAN PROVERB

What a wave of grateful coolness the ice and its yet more seductive sister, ice-cream, contribute when the dog-star reigns and cicadas have begun to shrill. Who among the calumniators of sweets would wish them banished in support of a fallacious theory that sweetmeats render woman more capricious, and are injurious to the roses and lilies of her skin? —GEORGE ELLWANGER

I was presented . . . with a card on which some thirty different types of ices were listed. The temptation was atrocious. My soul responds to a mere vanilla ice cream smeared out

into the thick glass of an Italian ice-cream vendor; but here was an opportunity to sample ices which were to the ordinary vanilla as Hyperion to a satyr. Although I knew nothing could be worse for my complaint . . . I do not remember that ever in my life I was so anxious to make a right choice.
—COMPTON MACKENZIE

I don't think a really good pie can be made without a dozen or so children peeking over your shoulder as you stoop to look in at it every little while.   —JOHN GOULD

After dinner everyone moved to the drawing room, where two tables were set with sweets. On one table was an elaborate china set for dry preserves sitting on a gilt tray painted with brightly colored flowers. The set consisted of oblong little china drawers sliding in and out of china partitions. Each drawer was filled with candied fruits—raspberries, wild strawberries, and blackberries. The central, round box contained dried rose petals.   —SERGEI AKSAKOV

> They fetched him first the sweetest wine,
> Then mead in mazers they combine
>   With lots of royal spice,
> And gingerbread, exceeding fine,
> And liquorice and eglantyne
>   And sugar, very nice.
>
> —CHAUCER

She makes two, three, four, even five new desserts in a day. A light almond dacquoise is—as much as anything—the standard, the set piece, from which her work takes off on its travels through the stars. The dacquoise resembles cake and puts up a light crunchy resistance before it effects a melting disappearance between tongue and palate and a swift transduction through the bloodstream to alight in the brain as a poem.

—ANONYMOUS PASTRY CHEF, quoted by John McPhee

The dessert is said to be to the dinner what the madrigal is to literature—it is the light poetry of the kitchen.

—GEORGE ELLWANGER

Table Manners

The man in evening clothes dining with the napkin in his lap will eat only half as much food as a diner in evening clothes with his napkin in his collar. The former will not only be worrying about spotting his shirt bosom but about the remarks his wife will make if he does.

—DAMON RUNYON

Frankly, in our experience, when our pals sit down at a dining-room table set with matching china and matching silverware on a white tablecloth, they come under the shadow of a penal dining code learned in childhood. In the kitchen or out on the porch, they can be about fifty-percent funnier than at the table, where they sit up straighter and their conversation takes a turn toward higher ground—into the realm of issues and problems, needs and priorities.

—GARRISON KEILLOR

The Duc de Bourgogne [Louis XIV's grandson] and his two brothers had been taught the polite innovation of using a fork to eat with. But when they were invited to the King's table at supper, he would have none of it and forbade them to use such an instrument. He would never have had occasion to reproach me in the matter, for I have never in my life used anything to eat with but my knife and my fingers.
—PRINCESS PALATINE, sister-in-law to Louis XIV

When the ducks and the green peas came we looked at each other with dismay; we had only two-pronged, black-handled forks. It is true, the steel was bright as silver; but what were we to do? Miss Matty picked up her peas, one by one, on the point of the prongs, much as Amine ate her grains of rice after her previous feast with the Ghoul. Miss Pole sighed over her delicate young peas as she left them on one side of her plate untasted; for they *would* drop between the prongs. I looked at my host: the peas were going wholesale into his capacious mouth, shovelled up by his large rounded knife. I saw, I imitated, I survived! —E. S. GASKELL

Table
Manners

The frightful manner of feeding with their knives, till the whole blade seemed to enter into the mouth; and the still more frightful manner of cleaning the teeth afterwards with a pocket-knife. —FRANCES TROLLOPE

> We could not lead a pleasant life,
> And 'twould be finished soon,
> If peas were eaten with the knife,
> And gravy with the spoon.
> Eat slowly: only men in rags
> And gluttons old in sin
> Mistake themselves for carpet bags
> And tumble victuals in.
> —SIR WALTER RALEIGH

During the week we did not bother much about knives and forks and tablecloths. A big plate of herring or other fish was set in the middle of the table, along with a dish of potatoes, and we simply stretched out our hands. —EDWIN MUIR

The three great stumbling blocks in a girl's education, she says, are *homard a l'Americaine,* a boiled egg, and asparagus.

Shoddy table manners, she says, have broken up many a happy home.   —COLETTE

Good manners: The noise you don't make when you're eating soup.   —BENNETT CERF

Jean won me over with his good manners—especially the way he handled his mullet, baked and served whole, naturally including the head. He carved the fish with a surgeon's precision, removing the bones as perfectly as any maître d'hôtel could have. These things were and are terribly important to me—the signs of breeding and good manners.
—SIMONE BECK

I'd discovered, after a lot of extreme apprehension about what spoons to use, that if you do something incorrect at table with a certain arrogance, as if you knew perfectly well you were doing it properly, you can get away with it and nobody will think you are bad-mannered or poorly brought up. They will think you are original and very witty.
—SYLVIA PLATH

When you sit down you should immediately put a napkin around your neck and then, very slowly, reach for the carafe of vodka. Now you don't pour the dear stuff into any old glass . . . oh no! You must pour it into an antediluvian glass made of silver, one which belonged to your grandfather, or into a pot-bellied glass bearing the inscription "Even Monks Imbibe!" And you don't drink the vodka down right away. No, sir. First you take a deep breath, wipe your hands, and glance up at the ceiling to demonstrate your indifference.

Only then do you raise that vodka slowly to your lips and suddenly—sparks! They fly from your stomach to the furthest reaches of your body. —ANTON CHEKHOV

In carving a partridge I splashed her with gravy from head to foot; and though I saw three distinct brown rills of animal juice trickling down her cheek, she had the complaisance to swear that not a drop had reached her. Such circumstances are the triumphs of civilized life. —SYDNEY SMITH

Ah gentlemen, keep a little quiet, one does not know what one is eating. —MONTMAUR

Taking Tea

Tea began as a medicine and grew into a beverage. In China, in the eighth century, it entered the realm of poetry as one of the polite amusements. The fifteenth century saw Japan ennoble it into a religion of aestheticism—Teaism. Teaism is a cult founded on the adoration of the beautiful among the sordid facts of everyday existence. It inculcates purity and harmony, the mystery of mutual charity, the romanticism of the social order. It is essentially a worship of the Imperfect, as it is a tender attempt to accomplish something possible in this impossible thing we know as life. . . . It is hygiene, for it enforces cleanliness; it is economics, for it shows com-

fort in simplicity rather than in the complex and costly; it is moral geometry, inasmuch as it defines our sense of proportion to the universe. —KAKUZO OKAKURA

The best tea is drunk in St. Petersburg and generally throughout Russia. Since China has a common border with Siberia, tea need not be transported by water to reach Moscow or St. Petersburg. Sea voyages are very bad for tea.
—ALEXANDRE DUMAS

The height of luxury was reached in the winter afternoons . . . lying in a tin bath in front of a coal fire, drinking tea, and eating well-buttered crumpets is an experience few can have today. —J. C. MASTERMAN

"Oh, for a good cup of tea!" A truly British cry that I echo so often in my travels around four o'clock in the afternoon. Tea is my panacea, my consolation—if you will, my "fix." —DIANA KENNEDY

Our trouble is that we drink too much tea. I see in this the slow revenge of the Orient, which has diverted the Yellow River down our throats. —J. B. PRIESTLEY

Tea! thou soft, thou sober, sage, and venerable liquid, thou female tongue-running, smile-soothing, heart-opening, wink-tippling cordial, to whose glorious insipidity I owe the happiest moments of my life, let me fall prostrate. —COLLEY CIBBER

If you are cold, tea will warm you—if you are too heated, it will cool you—if you are depressed, it will cheer you—if you are excited, it will calm you. —WILLIAM GLADSTONE

> Now stir the fire, and close the shutters fast,
> Let fall the curtains, wheel the sofa round,
> And, while the bubbling and loud hissing urn
> Throws up a steamy column, and the cups,
> That cheer but not inebriate, wait on each,
> So let us welcome peaceful ev'ning in.
> —WILLIAM COWPER

Retired to tea and scandal, according to their ancient custom. —WILLIAM CONGREVE

Thank God for tea! What would the world do without tea!
How did it exist? I am glad I was not born before tea!
                                                —SYDNEY SMITH

Tea, though ridiculed by those who are naturally coarse in
their nervous sensibilities . . . will always be the favourite
beverage of the intellectual.   —THOMAS DE QUINCEY

    We had a kettle: we let it leak:
        Our not repairing it made it worse.
    We haven't had any tea for a week . . .
        The bottom is out of the Universe!
                                                —RUDYARD KIPLING

There are few hours in life more agreeable than the hour
dedicated to the ceremony known as afternoon tea.
                                                —HENRY JAMES

The iron kettle would be singing as it hung from its hook
over the kitchen fire, the clock ticking on the wall, a white
cloth spread on the table for our tea, a loaf from our weekly
batch, butter from one or other of the neighboring farms
marked in the pretty lozenge-shaped pattern traditional in
the neighborhood, our own raspberry jam, in a ruby glass
jam-dish; my glass of milk set aside from the morning on
the cold slab of the larder, its cream a band at the top,
narrower or wider as the cow was newly calved or going
dry.   —KATHLEEN RAINE

Love and scandal are the best sweeteners of tea.

—HENRY FIELDING

A tea table without a big cake in the country in England would look very bare and penurious. The ideal table should include some sort of hot buttered toast or scone, one or two sorts of sandwiches, a plate of small light cakes and our friend the luncheon cake. Add a pot of jam or honey, and a plate of brown and white bread and butter—which I implore my readers not to cut too thin—and every eye will sparkle, and all those wishing to follow the fashionable craze of slimming will groan in despair.

—LADY SYSONBY, *Lady Sysonby's Cookbook*

In Russia a custom startling to strangers is that men drink tea in glasses and women in china cups. Here is the legend behind this custom. It seems that teacups were first made in Kronstadt, and the bottom was decorated with a view of that city. When a teahouse proprietor stinted on the tea, this picture could be seen clearly, and the customer would say to him "I can see Kronstadt." Since the proprietor could not deny this, he was caught *in flagrante delicto*. It became customary, then, for tea to be served in teahouses in glasses, at the bottom of which there was nothing to see, let alone Kronstadt!   —ALEXANDRE DUMAS

Day faded: on the table, glowing, the samovar of evening boiled, and warmed the Chinese teapot; flowing beneath it, vapour wreathed and coiled. Already Olga's hand was

gripping the urn of perfumed tea, and tipping into the cups
its darkling stream—meanwhile a boy handed cream.

—ALEXANDER PUSHKIN

By the time we arrived home, the tea trolley was laid ready
in front of the fire. We would sit close to the flames to warm
ourselves. When it was time to toast the crumpets or currant
buns, the logs were pushed back to reveal the glowing coals.
The brass toasting fork that Father used to polish with vigor
each Sunday morning was taken down from its place by the
chimney and whatever was to be toasted impaled—if there
had been roast beef for lunch, then we would toast thick
slices of bread and slather them with drippings from the
roasting pan. We were not allowed to start with cake: watercress or fish-paste sandwiches, or bread and butter, or
scones and jam had to be eaten in quantity before we were
allowed to go on to the sweet things. There was a round,
layered plate rack on the table to hold the small cakes: coco-
nut pyramids; maids of honor—tartlets of puff pastry filled
with almond paste and apricot jam; Banbury cakes; Shrews-
bury biscuits—all made at home. On separate plates covered
with crocheted doilies were the large round cakes. There
were usually three to choose from: a gingerbread, a rather
dry seed cake, gritty with whole caraway seeds that I
intensely disliked, and a chocolate Swiss roll (jelly roll) filled
with real whipped cream or a Dundee cake with its pattern
of toasted almond halves over the top. And this, mind you,
was ordinary tea, not high tea. High tea takes place from
five o'clock on, a sort of tea-cum-supper when something
savory, hot or cold, is served.   —DIANA KENNEDY

Truffles

Your truffles must come to the table in their own stock. Do not stint when you serve yourself: the truffle is an appetite creator, an aid to digestion. And as you break open this jewel sprung from a poverty-stricken soil, imagine—if you have never visited it—the desolate kingdom where it rules. For it kills the dog rose, drains life from the oak, ripens beneath an ungrateful bed of pebbles. —COLETTE

The truffle is not an outright aphrodisiac, but it may in certain circumstances make women more affectionate and men more amiable. —BRILLAT-SAVARIN

Presently we were aware of an odour gradually coming towards us, something musky, fiery, savoury, mysterious—a hot, drowsy smell, that lulls the senses and yet enflames them—the truffles were coming. —W. M. THACKERAY

If I can't have too many truffles, I'll do without truffles.
—COLETTE

Upstairs, Downstairs

On Sundays and holiday a gigantic pie was baked. The gentry ate it for the first two days, the servants were allowed to eat it on the third and fourth days, and on the fifth day the last stale remnants, devoid of stuffing, were given as a special favor to Antip. —IVAN GONCHAROV

The cookshop in Venice opens upon you at almost every turn . . . and looking in, you see its vast heaps of frying fish, and its huge caldrons of ever-boiling broth which smell to heaven with garlic and onions. In the seducing windows smoke golden mountains of polenta (a thicker kind of mush or hasty-pudding, made of Indian meal, and universally eaten in North Italy), platters of crisp minnows, bowls of rice, roast poultry, dishes of snails and liver; and around the fascinating walls hang huge plates of bronzed earthenware for a lavish and hospitable show, and for the representation of those scenes of Venetian story which are modeled upon them in bas-relief. Here I like to take my unknown friend—my scoundrel facchino or rascal gondolier—as he comes to buy his dinner, and bargains eloquently with the cook, who stands with a huge ladle in his hand capable of skimming mysterious things from vasty depths. I am spellbound by the drama which ensues, and in which all the chords of the human heart are touched, from those that tremble at high tragedy, to those that are shaken by broad farce. When the diner has bought his dinner, and issues forth with his polenta in one hand, and his fried minnows or stewed snails in the other, my fancy fondly follows him to his gondola-station, where he eats it, and quarrels volubly with other gondoliers across the grand canal.

—WILLIAM DEAN HOWELLS

Carving up a whole animal, whether a chicken or an ox, has from time immemorial expressed not only family feeling and cohesion among people sharing that animal, but also hierarchy and difference. In ancient Greece, for example, an animal eaten in common was a symbol of the organization of the group, and indeed of society itself, in its diversity as well as its wholeness. A pig or an ox has only four legs, one liver, two haunches, and so on: it is impossible for everyone to receive the same cut of meat. Many traditions have assigned status to various cuts; it mattered deeply which piece you got, and it usually fell to the head man to be the carver, who "did the honours" and assigned to each person his "portion," which could be broadly representative of his kinship or friendship status, and of his lot in life.

—MARGARET VISSER

Not only were the kitchen and the servants' hall never visited by my mother, but they stood as far removed from her consciousness as if they were the corresponding quarters in a hotel. My father had no inclination, either, to run the house. But he did order the meals. With a little sigh, he would open a kind of album laid by the butler on the dinner table after dessert and in his elegant, flowing hand, write down the menu for the following day. He had a peculiar habit of letting his pencil or fountain pen vibrate just above the paper while he pondered the next ripple of words. My mother nodded a vague consent to his suggestions or made a wry face.

—VLADIMIR NABOKOV

Vegetables

Ripe 'Sparagrass
Fit for Lad or Lass
To make their Water pass
'Tis a pretty Picking
With a tender Chicken
—JONATHAN SWIFT

I have this image of early summer, May and June. We walk home slowly up the village street, which runs across the cliff at a kindly slope. The midday angelus rings from the church tower above us. Children stream out of school, flow politely past our slower feet into open cottage doors. The air pulses with the warm smell of lilac, but as we pass each door, the lilac dominance is subdued by heady wafts of asparagus cooking. —JANE GRIGSON

With fresh asparagus, the higher your income the higher up the stalk you cut off the tip. —BILL RATHJE

And God said: Behold I have given you every herb-bearing seed upon the earth, and all the trees that have in themselves seed of their own kind, to be your meat.
—GENESIS 1:29

The near end of the street was rather dark and had mostly vegetable shops. Abundance of vegetables—piles of white and green fennel, like celery, and great sheaves of young, purplish, sea-dust-coloured artichokes, nodding their buds, piles of great radishes, scarlet and bluey purple, carrots, long strings of dried figs, mountains of big oranges, scarlet large peppers, a large slice of pumpkin, a great mass of colours and vegetable freshnesses. —D. H. LAWRENCE

Eating an artichoke is like getting to know someone really well. —WILLI HASTINGS

Large, naked, raw carrots are acceptable as food only to those who live in hutches eagerly awaiting Easter.
—FRAN LEBOWITZ

Honey underground
Is the winter carrot
Between St. Andrew's Day and Christmas.
—OLD GAELIC RHYME

Cabbage, n: A familiar kitchen-garden vegetable about as large and wise as a man's head. —AMBROSE BIERCE

Cabbages, whose heads, tightly folded, see and hear nothing of this world, dreaming only on the yellow and green magnificence that is hardening within them.

—JOHN HAINES

My brother Nikolai, sitting in his government office, dreamed of how he would eat his own cabbages, which would fill the whole yard with such a savory smell, take his meals on the green grass, sleep in the sun.

—ANTON CHEKHOV

What I say is that, if a fellow really likes potatoes, he must be a pretty decent sort of fellow. —A. A. MILNE

If beef's the King of Meat, potato's the Queen of the Garden World. —IRISH SAYING

I have no truck with lettuce, cabbage, and similar chlorophyll. Any dietician will tell you that a running foot of apple strudel contains four times the vitamins of a bushel of beans.

—S. J. PERELMAN

Spinach is the broom of the stomach. —FRENCH PROVERB

There is no dignity in the bean. Corn, with no affectation of superiority, is, however, the child of song. It waves in all literature. But mix it with beans, and its high tone is gone. Succotash is vulgar.   —CHARLES DUDLEY WARNER

Abstain from beans.   —PYTHAGORAS

Abstain from beans. There be sundry interpretations of this symbol. But Plutarch and Cicero think beans to be forbidden of Pythagoras, because they be windy and do engender impure humours and for that cause provoke bodily lust.
—RICHARD TAVERNER

From the United States every year a kind friend sent a little packet of sweet-corn seed grown and gathered by his mother. It was a great treat for us. At that time there was no table corn in France. The French grew corn for animals— in the Bugey, for the chickens. When it was known that we were growing it and eating it, they considered us savages. No one was seduced by the young ears we gave them to taste.   —ALICE B. TOKLAS

Corn by the common usage is eaten from the cob, but the exhibition is not interesting.
—*GENTLE MANNERS, A GUIDE TO GOOD MORALS*,
a Shaker publication

The artichoke above all is a vegetable expression of civilised living, of the long view, of increasing delight by anticipation and crescendo. No wonder it was once regarded as an aphrodisiac. It had no place in the troll's world of instant gratification. It makes no appeal to the meat-and-two-veg. mentality. —JANE GRIGSON

I stick to asparagus which still seems to inspire gentle thought. —CHARLES LAMB

Eating cress makes one witty. —GREEK PROVERB

> For pottage and puddings and custards and pies
> Our pumpkins and parsnips are common supplies;
> We have pumpkin at morning and pumpkin at noon,
> If it was not for pumpkin, we should be undone.
> —AMERICAN FOLKSONG, C. 1630

Asparagus: There are three varieties, white, violet, and green. The white is the earliest. Its flavour is mild and pleasant, but it has little substance. The violet is the thickest and most substantial. The green is thinner, but more of it is edible. It has a fine flavour. In Italy where taste is stronger than refined, the wild asparagus is preferred. The best way to prepare asparagus is by steaming. The Romans had a saying when they wanted something done quickly. "Do it," they said, "in less time than it takes to cook asparagus."
—ALEXANDRE DUMAS

At the end of this month one sees the points of asparagus
emerge, something which brings a great consolation to those
who, tired of potatoes and dried cereals, long for something
green.   —Grimod de La Reynière

The beet is the most intense of vegetables. The radish,
admittedly, is more feverish, but the fire of the radish is a
cold fire, the fire of discontent not of passion. Tomatoes are
lusty enough, yet there runs through tomatoes an undercur-
rent of frivolity. Beets are deadly serious.   —Tom Robbins

The ashes for the potatoes reposed in an urn, as if they
were the ashes of a hero. By urn I mean a three-legged black
cast-iron kettle, standing high on its outspread legs and provided with a convex lid with one sole flange. Seeing it at a
distance in the gloom, one thought, "What is that strange
animal?" In the ashes it contained, fine grayish-white and
sifted ashes, we carefully buried a few big unpeeled potatoes, then planted the whole thing in the glowing coals,
over which we heaped more ashes. Cooked without water
or steam, the potatoes became marvelously "floury"; you
needed only to add some fresh butter and a pinch of salt.
Under their powdery skin I found both the main course and
the dessert, for I also mixed in with their crumbly flesh some

very sweet apple sauce. In the same way, we cooked those beetroots that go so well with lamb's lettuce in a salad.

—COLETTE

No vegetable exists which is not better slightly undercooked.

—JAMES BEARD

The cooking of a vegetable is the transformation of a given object without consciousness into another object equally devoid of consciousness. —JEAN-PAUL SARTRE

Vegetarians

Vegetables are interesting but lack a sense of purpose when unaccompanied by a good cut of meat. —FRAN LEBOWITZ

I won't eat anything that has intelligent life, but I'd gladly eat a network executive or a politician. —MARTY FELDMAN

Vegetarians claim to be immune from most diseases but they have been known to die from time to time . . . there are millions of vegetarians in the world but only one George Bernard Shaw. You do not obtain eminence so cheaply as by eating macaroni instead of mutton chops.

—GEORGE BERNARD SHAW

I have no doubt that it is part of the destiny of the human race, in its gradual improvement, to leave off eating animals, as surely as the savage tribes have left off eating each other when they came in contact with each other.

—HENRY DAVID THOREAU

It is beneficial to one's health not to be carnivorous. The strongest animals, such as the bull, are vegetarians. Look at me. I have ten times as much good health and energy as a meat-eater.

—GEORGE BERNARD SHAW

Vegetarians have wicked, shifty eyes, and laugh in a cold calculating manner. They pinch little children, steal stamps, drink water, favor beards.

—J. B. MORTON

> You will find me drinking gin
> In the lowest kind of inn,
> Because I am a rigid vegetarian.

—G. K. CHESTERTON

Vegetarianism is harmless enough, though it is apt to fill a man with wind and self-righteousness.

—SIR ROBERT HUTCHINSON

There is no disease, bodily or mental, which adoption of vegetable diet, and pure water has not infallibly mitigated, wherever the experiment has been fairly tried.

—PERCY BYSSHE SHELLEY

My hearse will be followed not by mourning coaches but by herds of oxen, sheep, swine, flocks of poultry and a small travelling aquarium of live fish, all wearing white scarves in honor of the man who perished rather than eat his fellow creatures. —GEORGE BERNARD SHAW

Water, Water

Water is the best of all things. —PINDAR

The natural, temperate and necessary beverage for the thirsty is water. —CLEMENT OF ALEXANDRIA

The greatest necessity of the soldier is water.
—NAPOLEON I

Water is the only drink for a wise man.
—HENRY DAVID THOREAU

Water taken in moderation cannot hurt anybody.
—MARK TWAIN

It's all right to drink like a fish—if you drink what a fish drinks. —MARY PETTIBONE POOLE

What's for Lunch?

There he got out the luncheon-basket and packed a simple meal, in which, remembering the stranger's origin and preferences, he took care to include a yard of long French bread, a sausage out of which garlic sang, some cheese which lay down and cried, and a long-necked straw-covered flask wherein lay bottled sunshine shed and garnered on far Southern slopes. —KENNETH GRAHAME

The lunch on this occasion had begun with soles, sunk in a deep dish, over which the college cook had spread a counterpane of the whitest cream, save that it was branded here and there with brown spots like the spots on the flanks of a doe. After that came the partridges . . . many and various . . . with all their retinue of sauces and salads, the sharp and the sweet, each in its order; their potatoes, thin as coins but not so hard; their sprouts, foliated as rose-buds but more succulent. And no sooner had the roast and its retinue been done with than the silent serving man . . . set before us, wreathed in napkins, a confection which rose all sugar from the waves. —VIRGINIA WOOLF

As I was the host at luncheon I . . . said to the interpreter that if it was the religion of His Majesty [Ibn Saud] to deprive himself of smoking and alcohol I must point out

that my rule of life prescribed as an absolutely sacred rite
smoking cigars and also the drinking of alcohol before, after,
and if need be during all meals and in the intervals between
them.   —WINSTON CHURCHILL

Sunday lunch at the Pelletiers' runs from noon till three or
four in the afternoon when there is company. It begins with
fresh foie gras and Fernande's foie-gras pâté, and then, if it
is the mushroom season, there is a gratin of *cèpes* and maybe
a mushroom tart, too, and afterward one of Fernande's fat
ducks or a corn-fed chicken from the yard, and cheese, of
course, and the glazed apple turnover from her grandmother's recipe book (which is often charred now that Fernande
is teaching Clémentine (to make it) and an ice-cream bombe
with two flavors in the middle. There is wine from the *cave*,
and, after dessert, cognac and Armagnac and coffee and,
always, a plate of ordinary chocolates that Fernande drives
all the way to Brive to buy at the confectioner's, and, being
the only part of the meal she pays for, are what she assumes
has made it special.   —JANE KRAMER

When ordering lunch the big executives are just as indeci-
sive as the rest of us.   —WILLIAM FEATHER

By any standards we were still very poor and I still made
such small economies as saying that I had been asked out
to lunch and then spending two hours walking in the Lux-
embourg gardens and coming back to describe the marvel-

ous lunch to my wife. When you are twenty-five and are a natural heavyweight, missing a meal makes you very hungry. But it also sharpens all of your perceptions.

—ERNEST HEMINGWAY

What contemptible scoundrel stole the cork from my lunch?

—W. C. FIELDS

When We Were Young

What is patriotism but the love of good things we ate in our childhood.

—LIN YUTANG

"There's no such thing as bad food," Mama used to say. "There are only spoiled-rotten children."

—SAM LEVENSON

When I was young and poor, my favorite dish was caviar accompanied by a half bottle of Bollinger. But repetition destroys any pleasure, gastronomic or sexual, and now I have no favorite dish having eliminated all my "favorites"! Now I like nothing better than a bowl of well-

234

Writing
and
Read-
ing
About
Food

made Scottish porridge, accompanied by a glass of good sweet milk, "supped" in spoonfuls in turn. Delicious, good and nourishing and without after-effects.   —A. J. CRONIN

When a man is small, he loves and hates food with a ferocity which soon dims. At six years old his very bowels will heave when such a dish as creamed carrots or cold tapioca appears before him. His throat will close, and spots of nausea and rage swim in his vision. It is hard, later, to remember why, but at the time there is no pose in his disgust. He cannot eat; he says, "To hell with it!"   —M.F.K. FISHER

Writing and Reading About Food

Next to eating good dinners, a healthy man with a benevolent turn of mind, must like, I think, to read about them.
—WILLIAM M. THACKERAY

There is a communion of more than our bodies when bread is broken and wine is drunk. And that is my answer, when people ask me: Why do you write about hunger, and not wars or love.   —M.F.K. FISHER

No restaurants. The means of consoling oneself: reading cookbooks. —BAUDELAIRE

235

Writing
and
Read-
ing
About
Food

The trouble with most cookbooks is that they assume that people live the way they don't live. —MRS. APPLEYARD

The tome was a backbreaking thousand-odd pages thick and generously larded with color plates of presumably edible rococo and byzantine ornamentation, any subject of which would have taken a fairly accomplished home cook, working with tweezers and magnifying glass, a month to replicate.
—JAY JACOBS

And now with some pleasure I find that it's seven; and must cook dinner. Haddock and sausage meat. I think it is true that one gains a certain hold on sausage and haddock by writing them down. —VIRGINIA WOOLF

Hors d'oeuvre means "outside the meal" and regardless of how many different sorts may be provided "outside" or before any one meal, there is but one meal or *oeuvre*, so that, in French, *oeuvre* remains in the singular and *hors d'oeuvre* never is written hors d'oeuvres. —ANDRÉ SIMON

The word "gourmet" has been run into the ground. Anybody's cousin who drinks wine with his meals, or who substitutes broccoli for potatoes considers himself a gourmet. It's become a dreaded word in the American language.
—JAMES BEARD

236

Writing
and
Read-
ing
About
Food

Anyone who eats three meals a day should understand why cookbooks outsell sex books three to one.   —L. M. Boyd

The two biggest sellers in any bookstore are the cookbooks and the diet books. The cookbooks tell you how to prepare the food and the diet books tell you how not to eat any of it.   —Andy Rooney

Anyone who wants to write about food would do well to stay away from similes and metaphors, because if you're not careful, expressions like "light as a feather" make their way into your sentences, and then where are you?
                                        —Nora Ephron

> At the end of a sentence I call for tea
> At the end of a paragraph, bread and b.
> At the end of a page chip potatoes and hake
> At the end of a chapter fillet steak
>
> But ah! when I finish the ultimate line
> When I've brought to fulfillment the grand design
> When I look at the thing and it's mine all mine
> Then it's Oysters, my love, with Cold White Wine!
>   —Jan Morris

The primary requisite for writing well about food is a good appetite.   —A. J. Liebling

X-Rated Food

Ceres presents a plate of vermicelli,—
For love must be sustained like flesh and blood,—
While Bacchus pours out wine, or hands a jelly:
Eggs, oysters, too, are amatory food.
                                        —LORD BYRON

Red bordeaux is like the lawful wife: an excellent beverage
that goes with every dish and enables one to enjoy one's
food. But now and then a man wants a change, and champagne is the most complete and exhilarating change . . . it
is like a woman of the streets: everyone that can afford it
tries it sooner or later, but it has no real attraction. Moselle
is like the girl of fourteen to eighteen: light, quick on the
tongue, with an exquisite, evanescent perfume, but little
body. It may be used constantly and in quantities, but it
must be taken young.   —FRANK HARRIS

Let the goyim sink their teeth into whatever lowly creature crawls and grunts across the face of the dirty earth, we will not contaminate our humanity thus. Let them . . . gorge themselves upon anything and everything that moves, no matter how odious and abject the animal, no matter how grotesque or schmutzig or dumb. . . . Let them eat eels and frogs and pigs and crabs and lobsters; let them eat vulture, let them eat ape-meat and skunk if they like—a diet of abominable creatures well befits a breed of mankind so hopelessly shallow and empty-headed as to drink, to divorce, and to fight with their fists. . . . Thus saith the kosher laws, and who am I to argue that they're wrong. For look at Alex himself . . . sucks one night at a lobster's claw and within the hour his cock is out and aimed at a shikse on a Public Service bus. And his superior Jewish brain might as well be made of matzoh brei!   —PHILIP ROTH

Dear Fotis, how daintily, how charmingly you stir that casserole: I love watching you wriggle your hips. And what a wonderful cook you are! The man whom you allow to poke his finger into your little casserole is the luckiest fellow alive. That sort of stew would tickle the most jaded palate.

                                                            —APULEIUS

Xanadu

For he on honey-dew hath fed,
And drunk the milk of Paradise.
                    —SAMUEL TAYLOR COLERIDGE

To eat the lotus of the Nile
And drink the poppies of Cathay.
                    —WHITTIER

There would have to be bread, some rich, whole-grain bread and zwieback, and perhaps on a long, narrow dish some pale Westphalian ham laced with strips of white fat like an evening sky with bands of clouds. There would be some tea ready to be drunk, yellowish golden tea in glasses with silver saucers, giving off a faint fragrance. . . . Huge lemons, cut in slices, would sink like setting suns into the dusky sea, softly illuminating it with their radiating membranes, and its clear, smooth surface aquiver from the rising bitter essence.   —RAINER MARIA RILKE

A loaf of bread, a jug of wine, and $65 thou.
                    —ALAN KOEHLER

In Paradise . . . he will be waited on by 300 attendants while he eats, and shall be served in dishes of gold, whereof 300 shall be set before him at once, containing each a different kind of food, the last morsel of which shall be as grateful as the first, and will also be supplied with many sorts of liquors in vessels of the same metal; and to complete the entertainment, there will be no want of wine, which, though forbidden in this life, will yet be freely allowed in the next without danger, since the wine of Paradise will never inebriate though you drink it forever. —THE KORAN

In the deep south, mint juleps are not really drunk much. In fact, they are drunk so seldom that when, say, on Derby Day somebody gives a julep party, people drink them like cocktails, forgetting that a good julep holds at least five ounces of bourbon. Men fall facedown unconscious, women wander in the woods disconsolate and amnesiac, full of thoughts of Kahlil Gibran and the limberlost.

—WALKER PERCY

You Are What You Eat

Tell me what you eat and I will tell you what you are.
—BRILLAT-SAVARIN

I often wonder whether Brillat-Savarin's grand bluff was ever called. —JAY JACOBS

It's a very odd thing—
As odd as can be—
That whatever Miss T. eats
Turns into Miss T.
Porridge and apples,
Mince, muffins and mutton,
Jam, junket and jumbles—

Not a rap, not a button
It matters; the moment
They're out of her plate . . .
Whatever Miss T. eats
Turns into Miss T.
—WALTER DE LA MARE

Everything you see I owe to spaghetti.   —SOPHIA LOREN

Zakuski

Myself, I like the name zakuski, although I don't know why, for I have never had them in the classical way, countless bowls and dishes and platters set out upon a long table, to be tasted as and how I wished, and swept down with frequent little glasses of vodka. —M.F.K. FISHER

"That is caviar," she explained to him, "and this is vodka, the drink of the people, but I think you will find that the two are admirably suited to each other." —C. S. FORESTER

Dinner was served, and Mama noted that the table service was of solid gold. The *zakuski* came first and consisted of a

Russian silver bowl containing fresh sterlet caviar set in a larger bowl of crushed ice. This was accompanied by separate small dishes of chopped egg white and finely minced onion and was served with lemon wedges and thin slices of toast. *Les oeufs Fabergé* were next. These were eggs that had been hard-boiled, then carefully cut lengthwise. The egg had been combined with sautéed shallots and sour cream before being stuffed back into the shells, which were gold leafed and studded with tiny fake jewels. Both halves were put together and served, one to a guest, on a platter of brilliant green watercress. Then there were *siliotki v smetanye* (pickled herring dressed in sour cream), *salenye gribi* (pickled mushrooms), *ikra iz Baklajan* (eggplant caviar). With the *zakuski* tiny chilled glasses of vodka and Zubrokva were served.

—GEORGES SPUNT

Another good appetizer is stewed white mushrooms, with onion, you know, and bay leaf and other spices. You lift the lid off the dish, and the steam rises, a smell of mushrooms . . . sometimes it really brings tears to my eyes.

—ANTON CHEKHOV

INDEX OF AUTHORS